Servant of
Two Masters

BY CARLO GOLDONI

A NEW VERSION

by Tom Cone

SAMUEL FRENCH, INC.

45 WEST 25TH STREET	NEW YORK 10010
7623 SUNSET BOULEVARD	HOLLYWOOD 90046
LONDON	*TORONTO*

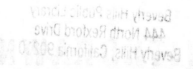

SERVANT OF TWO MASTERS was first produced by the Stratford
Festival, on the Avon Stage, in June, 1980, with the
following cast:

SMERALDINA	Jennifer Phipps
PANTALONE	Graham Campbell
LOMBARDI	Maurice Good
SILVIO	Rod Beattie
BRIGHELLA	Norman Browning
CLARICE	Barbara Budd
TRUFFALDINO	Lewis Gordon
BEATRICE	Goldie Semple
VITTORIO	John Cutts
NICKI	Stephen Ouimette
FLORINDO	Brent Carver

Directed by Peter Moss
Set by Michael Eagan
Costumes by Janice Lindsay

SERVANT OF TWO MASTERS was subsequently produced, in this
revised edition, at the Vancouver Playhouse, in September,
1980, with the following cast:

SMERALDINA	Nicola Cavendish
PANTALONE	Owen Foran
LOMBARDI	Peter Elliott
SLIVIO	Ron Halder
BRIGHELLA	Des Smiley
CLARICE	Michele Goodger
TRUFFALDINO	Tom Wood
BEATRICE	Diane D'Aquila
VITTORIO	Donald Adams
NICKI	Ross Imrie
FLORINDO	Richard Donat

Directed by Roger Hodgman
Designed by Cameron Porteous

The Characters:

PANTALONE	a Venetian merchant.
CLARICE	Pantalone's daughter
DR. LOMBARDI	a lawyer
SILVIO	Lombardi's son
BEATRICE RASPONI	
FLORINDO ARETUSI	Beatrice's lover
BRIGHELLA	an innkeeper
SMERALDINA	maidservant to Clarice
TRUFFALDINO	servant to Beatrice and Florindo
NICKI	a waiter
VITTORIO	a waiter (also doubles as a porter)

The Setting:

The play is set in Venice during the course of one day.

Special Thanks to:

Professor Carlo Chiarenza, Roger Hodgman, Urjo Kareda, Joyce Lannon, The New Play Centre, Jace Van der Veen and Tom Wood.

SERVANT OF TWO MASTERS

Act One, Scene One

Inside PANTALONE's house. SMERALDINA
rushes on with a duster. She is
frantically cleaning and humming a
passionate song to herself. As she
gets caught up in the humming she
suddenly exclaims:

SMERALDINA: Oh! (fanning herself with the duster) I've got to
                stop doing this to myself. They say love never dies.
                Mine has never lived. LUCIANO! But it will. It
                will. It better. LUCIANO! (backdrop is lowered)
                Thank you sweet boy! A little lower. We haven't had
                these tapestries in the house since the signora's
                funeral. A marvellous woman. I just wish her
                daughter had more of her traits. That's what this
                is all about. I didn't mention that? Oh. I'm sorry.
                We're about to have an engagement ceremony. The
                daughter I was speaking about. My lady. She's
                getting engaged to a boy...who...well, it's hard to
                believe. In fact, this is her second engagement. To
                a different man though. My lady is no fool. She
                never saw the other one. Too bad. Sounded
                interesting. Died. I think.

PANTALONE: Is everyone ready? Dr. Lombardi?

LOMBARDI: Coming, Signor Pantalone.

PANTALONE: Silvio?

LOMBARDI: Silvio?!

SILVIO: Yes, Father. I was just... I'm sorry Signor
                Pantalone.

PANTALONE: Stand there.

SILVIO: Here?

PANTALONE: That's right. And oh, look at that face. Is she ready? Stand next to your Silvio, Clarice. Good. Now Brighella.

BRIGHELLA: I'm here, Signor Pantalone.

PANTALONE: I know that, Brighella. Please. Stand alongside my daughter. Smeraldina? Will you join us please?

SMERALDINA: (aside) If you promise to join me with a husband.

PANTALONE: What's that?

SMERALDINA: Next to Master Brighella?

PANTALONE: Is everyone ready? Clarice?

CLARICE: Yes, Papa.

PANTALONE: Well then, let's begin. Remember. It is not a legality as yet. Although soon...

LOMBARDI: Legality?

PANTALONE: Absolutely not. Mind you it does suggest serious...

LOMBARDI: Intentions?

PANTALONE: Thank you.

LOMBARDI: You're welcome.

PANTALONE: Well?

LOMBARDI: Silvio?!

SILVIO: Yes, Father, I'm sorry. I was just...now? Oh my dear Clarice!

PANTALONE: No, no, no...

SMERALDINA: (aside) Yes! Yes! Yes!

PANTALONE: Let's save the intimacy, Silvio.

CLARICE: Papa!

SILVIO: Dear Clarice?

PANTALONE: Did I not make myself clear? Casually please, casually.

SILVIO:	Ummm...
SMERALDINA:	(aside) Just say it, Master Silvio!
SILVIO:	Clarice?
CLARICE:	Yes, Silvio?
SILVIO:	I ummm...promise to...
CLARICE:	Of course you do! I promise to be your wife and you promise to be my husband!
SILVIO:	Exactly!

(General celebration and applause)

CLARICE:	Is that it, Papa?
PANTALONE:	One moment. One moment. Now that we have actually come to an agreement and oh, how I remember my own agreement. Your stubborn grandfather made it very difficult for your mother and I, Clarice. He created several barriers for me to cross and cross I finally did. Ahh, but fate is with you, isn't it, Silvio?
SILVIO:	Always will be, sir!
PANTALONE:	As, it of course was with me. My only regret is that my future son-in-law has no interest in the reputable trade of mercantilism. A repectable and...
CLARICE:	I asked you, Papa?
PANTALONE:	I know, I know. Well, I...want to thank you for being witness to this umm...
LOMBARDI:	Engagement?
PANTALONE:	I suppose so.
BRIGHELLA:	My pleasure, sirs.
PANTALONE:	Smeraldina?
SMERALDINA:	(annoyed aside) Witness witness...
PANTALONE:	Smeraldina? Have you not witnessed?!
SMERALDINA:	Yes, thank you, sir.
PANTALONE:	Now I have completed our agreement, Brighella.

BRIGHELLA: Thank you, sir.

PANTALONE: I, of course was witness to your daughter's wedding, Brighella.

BRIGHELLA: It was an honour; sir.

PANTALONE: And now you are witness to mine. The good Dr. Lombardi shares my belief, however, that such sacred occasions are best celebrated within an intimate atmosphere.

LOMBARDI: Signor Pantalone?

PANTALONE: Yes, Dr. Lombardi?

LOMBARDI: You never did tell us what really happened to Signor Federigo Rasponi. The man your daughter was previously engaged to?

PANTALONE: Federigo Rasponi?

LOMBARDI: That is his name, isn't it?

PANTALONE: Yes, of course. Now?...

LOMBARDI: Why not?

PANTALONE: Oh, well...he died.

LOMBARDI: We knew that, sir.

PANTALONE: You are a lawyer, aren't you, Lombardi?

LOMBARDI: De facto I am, sir.

PANTALONE: He died for his sister. With a sword. That's all I know.

LOMBARDI: Isn't it amazing that my son's engagement would not have taken place if fate hadn't...

PANTALONE: We all know that, Dr. Lombardi.

BRIGHELLA: Signor Rasponi?

PANTALONE: You still here?

BRIGHELLA: Where did this happen, sir?

PANTALONE: Turin. Odd, in Turin, isn't it?

BRIGHELLA: I can't believe it!

PANTALONE: You knew Signor Rasponi, Brighella?

BRIGHELLA: I did, sir. I knew his sister as well.

PANTALONE: Worthy of such an act?

BRIGHELLA: A horsewoman, sir.

PANTALONE: What?

BRIGHELLA: He treasured her, sir.

PANTALONE: Obviously. Too bad. But not too bad for you, eh
                Clarice? Please, let's eat before our stomachs turn
                with these tragic deeds of honour. You know what
                I like, Brighella.

BRIGHELLA: Of course, Signor Pantalone. You know my reputation...

PANTALONE: No suprises, Brighella.

                         (A knock is heard at the door)

                Smeraldina? Smeraldina?!

SMERALDINA: Yes, sir?

PANTALONE: The door is knocking

SMERALDINA: It is? Really, sir? I'm going, sir. Right away.

CLARICE: Papa?

PANTALONE: How long have we had her?

CLARICE: May we go now?

PANTALONE: Of course, but let us see who this knocking is.

CLARICE: Papa! May we go now?

PANTALONE: Calm down, Clarice.

LOMBARDI: My Silvio will calm her down, sir.

TRUFFALDINO: (walking backwards and smiling at SMERALDINA) Hope
                to see you. Goodbye. (bumps into PANTALONE)

PANTALONE: Hello.

TRUFFALDINO: Hello.

PANTALONE: I'm sorry.

TRUFFALDINO:	That's all right! (aside) Do I detect the smell of clothes that are too new? Could I go so far as to say "nouveau riche"?
PANTALONE:	Yes?
TRUFFALDINO:	(gazing at CLARICE) Yes. But she's not bad.
PANTALONE:	That is my daughter, sir.
TRUFFALDINO:	Congratulations. (to SMERALDINA) And who are you?
SMERALDINA:	Smeraldina. The lady's maid.
TRUFFALDINO:	Congratulations to your lady.
LOMBARDI:	Who is this, sir?
PANTALONE:	What is it you want? Are you bringing something? And what is your name?
TRUFFALDINO:	All at once, sir?
PANTALONE:	Is this a fool? Or am I mistaken?
LOMBARDI:	There's strong evidence...
TRUFFALDINO:	Is this a celebration?
SMERALDINA:	I wish.
TRUFFALDINO:	Me too.
PANTALONE:	Will you please tell us who you are, sir?
SILVIO:	Now!
PANTALONE:	Silvio!
TRUFFALDINO:	Who, me?
PANTALONE:	No. Yes!
TRUFFALDINO:	A servant.
PANTALONE:	I know that.
TRUFFALDINO:	Oh...of my master.
PANTALONE:	And who is your master?
TRUFFALDINO:	A man who wishes to see Signor Pantalone.
PANTALONE:	Why am I doing this?

TRUFFALDINO: Are you Signor Pantalone?

PANTALONE: I am. And who is your master?

TRUFFALDINO: Signor Federigo Rasponi.

PANTALONE: Of Turin?

TRUFFALDINO: Very good sir. I myself am from Bergamo, sir.

PANTALONE: I am not interested in where you're from!

CLARICE: What are we going to do, Papa?

PANTALONE: Nothing!

CLARICE: Nothing?

SILVIO: Nothing?

LOMBARDI: Calm down, Silvio!

TRUFFALDINO: I am Truffaldino Battochio of Bergamo, sir. (aside)
              Poor gentleman. I'll have to repeat myself. I am
              Truffaldino Battochio! Signor Rasponi is waiting
              for you outside.

PANTALONE: Outside?

TRUFFALDINO: (to audience) Is my accent off? (to PANTALONE) He
              wishes to see you.

PANTALONE: Rasponi is dead!

TRUFFALDINO: NO!

PANTALONE: YES!

TRUFFALDINO: When? Oh, I shouldn't have left him. What am I
              going to do now? Please forgive me! What can I say?
              I must see this! (starts to exit, stops. To
              SMERALDINA) Don't go. (exits)

PANTALONE: What did he say?

LOMBARDI: Rasponi is here? My poor Silvio.

SILVIO: Precious Clarice!

PANTALONE: Please! Not now. You saw the letters, Clarice.
              He's dead.

SILVIO: And if he isn't?

TRUFFALDINO:	(enters) Do you take me for a fool, sir? Do I look like the type of person who speaks out of both sides of my mouth? Bergamo, sir. Remember Bergamo?
PANTALONE:	He's mad!
LOMBARDI:	I'm not so sure.
TRUFFALDINO:	My master.
ALL:	Yes?
TRUFFALDINO:	Signor Rasponi...
ALL:	Yes?
TRUFFALDINO:	(to audience) I feel like I'm conducting.
ALL:	YES?
TRUFFALDINO:	Is alive.
ALL:	NO!
TRUFFALDINO:	YES! All there. Awaiting your reply.
PANTALONE:	Rasponi of Turin?
TRUFFALDINO:	(aside) Not again.
LOMBARDI:	It may be worth investigating, Signor Pantalone. Bring your master to us, servant!
PANTALONE:	Yes. Let's see the tricks you've learned in Bergamo.
TRUFFALDINO:	Tricks.
PANTALONE:	Now! Awake the dead!
TRUFFALDINO:	(aside) Well, that'll be easy.
SMERALDINA:	Really?
TRUFFALDINO:	(to SMERALDINA) Trust me. (exits)
CLARICE:	What are we going to do?
SILVIO:	There's nothing to do. You're mine. That's it! That's all there is to it. If he's alive he's too late!
BRIGHELLA:	If it's really Rasponi, I'll be the one to identify him.

ANTALONE: Thank you, Brighella.

                    (BEATRICE enters dressed as a man)

EATRICE: Signor Pantalone dei Bisognosi?

                    (No response. Everyone is shocked. BEATRICE
                    extends her hand)

            Signor Federigo Rasponi... (no response) of Turin...
            (no response)

RUFFALDINO: (to SMERALDINA) See what I mean? (to PANTALONE) See
            what I mean?

ANTALONE: Yes. This is unbelievable. Brighella?!

RIGHELLA: (aside) Unbelievable, indeed.

ANTALONE: You claim to be here, sir?

EATRICE: I am here.

ANTALONE: Silent. Dr. Lombardi?

OMBARDI: Yes.

ANTALONE: I'm sorry, sir. We've just heard terrible news about
            you.

EATRICE: Ahhh. You're speaking of the duel.

ANTALONE: Yes. Something to do with your sister?

EATRICE: Killed in a duel perhaps?

ANTALONE: Right! No! Yes! No, I mean, you were killed in a
            duel. Not your sister.

EATRICE: Just wounded.

ANTALONE: She was?

EATRICE: I was.

ANTALONE: Oh I'm sorry to hear that.

EATRICE: So...here I am. Recovered and fulfilling our
            original agreement. I'm sure you'll excuse the delay.
            I know that a man like yourself will appreciate the
            hazards one has to overcome to keep the honour of
            one's own family intact.

PANTALONE: Umm...yes...yes...of course! But we have proof that.
               umm...

BEATRICE: Yes?

LOMBARDI: Proof of...sir?

PANTALONE: Thank you. Proof of Signor Federigo Rasponi's death.

BEATRICE: You doubt me, sir?

PANTALONE: Of course not. I'm sorry but you must understand...

BEATRICE: I do.

PANTALONE: You do?

BEATRICE: Yes. Proof is what you need. What father wouldn't
               want proof that his daughter is marrying the right
               man? Here are four separate signatures. Each
               provides proof of who I am.

LOMBARDI: Proof?

BEATRICE: Precisely. The letter you are reading now is
               signed by your personal bank manager. Do you not
               recognize the signature?

PANTALONE: Yes. Of course.

CLARICE: It's happened! Everything we feared, Silvio. Right
               up to the last moment.

SILVIO: There is nothing to fear. I will never give you up.

BEATRICE: (noticing BRIGHELLA) Oh...

                    (TRUFFALDINO kisses SMERALDINA's hand)

SMERALDINA: Oh! Do that again.

PANTALONE: Yes?

BEATRICE: Brighella?

PANTALONE: Oh right. (trying to read the letters) Brighella,
               you know Signor Rasponi, don't you?

BRIGHELLA: I do sir. Brighella Cavicchio of Turin, sir.

BEATRICE: Ahh yes.

                    (BEATRICE goes to BRIGHELLA. PANTALONE
                    reads on)

BEATRICE: How long have you been in Venice? I implore you, don't give me away. (out loud) Do you still?...

BRIGHELLA: I still keep an inn, sir. Now in Venice, sir. I am at your service if you wish, sir.

BEATRICE: What marvellous fortune. To stay with a friend from the past as I meet a friend from the future.

CLARICE: Papa, you've got to do something!

PANTALONE: Just let me finish.

CLARICE: But hurry.

PANTALONE: It's true.

BEATRICE: Please, sir. Ask Signor Brighella.

PANTALONE: It's true?

BRIGHELLA: I indeed recognize this person, sir.

PANTALONE: Then I welcome you, Signor Federigo Rasponi. My daughter...Clarice.

LOMBARDI: Just give me a moment.

BEATRICE: Madam.

CLARICE: Sir.

BEATRICE: A bit cool, Signor Pantalone.

SILVIO: And why not?!

BEATRICE: (to PANTALONE) I see. And who is this?

PANTALONE: My nephew!

SILVIO: I am?

BEATRICE: Nephew?

SILVIO: I am Silvio Lombardi. Son of the doctor standing next to you, sir.

BEATRICE: Oh, your brother? Good day, sir.

LOMBARDI: What? Oh, and to you, sir. But...

SILVIO: I am not his nephew, sir! I am the fiancé of Clarice dei Bisognosi.

BEATRICE: I beg your pardon?

SILVIO: Agreed upon and witnessed just before your stupid
               servant...

PANTALONE: Will you please be quiet, Silvio.

BEATRICE: But was she not promised to me?

PANTALONE: Yes, yes she was. But we...I believed the story
               of your death. So much so that I hastily, hastily
               promised my daughter Clarice to Signor Silvio
               Lombardi. And now here you are. Late because you
               were defending your sister's honour. Thus proving
               to Clarice that you are an honourable man. You must
               appreciate the position I am in, Silvio. Dr. Lombardi
               An agreement is an agreement. There was an agreement
               before our agreement and that agreement must take
               precedence.

LOMBARDI: It would seem to me, sir, that a man who had just
               defended his sister's honour would, ipso facto,
               appreciate another's honour in jeopardy?

BEATRICE: Are you in trouble?

LOMBARDI: Why no, I...

BEATRICE: Do you need some assistance?

LOMBARDI: Yes.

BEATRICE: From whom?

SILVIO: From you, sir. You have arrived too late. Clarice
               is mine!

PANTALONE: Silvio.

LOMBARDI: Good for you.

PANTALONE: Dr. Lombardi!

SILVIO: I am sure that Clarice will agree -- anyone and that
               includes her father who wishes to separate her from
               me will have to confront my ability as a...

BEATRICE: Not another duel?

SILVIO: I do mean this, sir!

LOMBARDI: You are too late, sir! Your agreement is broken.
               Clarice is my son's!

BEATRICE: I'm sorry?

LOMBARDI: Prior intemporara potior indure.

CLARICE: Never! Never! Never! (exits)

PANTALONE: What are you saying? Clarice? Come back or I'll...

BEATRICE: Do not punish her, sir. We must have pity.

SILVIO: It's you I have pity for, sir. Clarice! (exits)

LOMBARDI: Silvio! (exiting) Serio vententibus ossa. Bones to the latecomers!

PANTALONE: Bones to the latecomers?

BEATRICE: Signor Pantalone, in due time your daughter will come to appreciate what a good husband I can be. Now, if you don't mind, I would like to discuss my second reason for being here.

PANTALONE: The marriage settlement.

BEATRICE: If you don't mind.

PANTALONE: Of course, sir. It is all in order. I have your money and we will sign the agreement whenever you are ready.

BEATRICE: Very good. Now, if you'll excuse me, I'll follow Signor Brighella to his inn.

PANTALONE: Yes. Is there anything I can do for you?

BEATRICE: An advance would be appreciated. With crime increasing on the roads, I brought only a little money with me.

PANTALONE: It would be my pleasure. You are staying with Brighella?

BEATRICE: Yes. But I will send my servant for the advance. He's an honest man, eager to serve me. Trust him.

PANTALONE: Trust him?

BEATRICE: Try. He did tell the truth, sir.

PANTALONE: He did?

TRUFFALDINO: He did.

PANTALONE: Yes, he did. I will. I will.

SMERALDINA: (enters) Signor Pantalone?

PANTALONE: What is it?

SMERALDINA: Your daughter, Clarice?

PANTALONE: Oh, right!

SMERALDINA: I think you should speak with her, sir.

PANTALONE: Yes. I should. Please excuse me. I trust you'll be a good host to Signor Rasponi, Brighella?

BRIGHELLA: I will, sir.

PANTALONE: Good. Now I must attend to my poor Clarice.

                  (Exits with SMERALDINA)

BRIGHELLA: Now, Signora...

BEATRICE: Wait for me on the street, Truffaldino.

TRUFFALDINO: But you promised me lunch!

BEATRICE: I know! I know! Later.

TRUFFALDINO: (exiting and mumbling) Later, later.

BRIGHELLA: Now Signora Beatrice, what is going on here?

BEATRICE: Ssssh. Look at me Brighella. You trust me?

BRIGHELLA: I do.

BEATRICE: You know Florindo Aretusi is my lover.

BRIGHELLA: Yes I heard.

BEATRICE: My brother hated him. He tried to defend my honour. Florindo tried to defend our love. There was a duel.

BRIGHELLA: Your brother...

BEATRICE: ...is dead, Brighella.

BRIGHELLA: Signora Beatrice?!

BEATRICE: I heard Florindo fled to Venice. So, I disguised myself in my brother's clothes. God forgive me.

BEATRICE:	(cont'd) I must find him, Brighella. My brother had letters of credit and they'll prove my existence as him, which of course you are here to confirm.

(BRIGHELLA crosses himself)

With these I shall take Signor Pantalone's money and help Florindo. Wherever he is. Oh Lord, let him be here in Venice. Please Brighella! Be with me. Help me!

BRIGHELLA: I will, madam.

BEATRICE: Oh, thank you!

BRIGHELLA: But I will not be part of a scheme that will embezzle Signor Pantalone's money.

BEATRICE: Brighella! Am I not Federigo's legal heir?

BRIGHELLA: You are, madam. Then tell Signor Pantalone.

BEATRICE: Are you crazy? That's what I'm running from. Under the Venetian law, Signor Pantalone is my guardian until I marry.

BRIGHELLA: (aside) That's an odd law.

BEATRICE: But if I marry without his consent I'll never receive the money owed to my brother. And who would consent to my marrying my brother's murderer?

BRIGHELLA: I'd have to agree to that.

BEATRICE: I need my freedom. I must have it, Brighella. Please!

BRIGHELLA: Very well then.

BEATRICE: Oh bless you. Now can we go?

BRIGHELLA: One more thing, Signora Beatrice -- and please do not misunderstand -- where did you find this servant?

BEATRICE: Bergamo.

BRIGHELLA: Well, I know good servants are getting scarcer these days...but...

BEATRICE: I found him in a vineyard, Brighella...crying.

BRIGHELLA: Crying?

BEATRICE: "My darling, my darling." I of course identified with the poor man.

BRIGHELLA: With a Bergamese? (pause) Come, Signora.

BEATRICE: You had to be there, Brighella.

        (BEATRICE and BRIGHELLA exit)

Act One, Scene Two

Outside BRIGHELLA's inn. TRUFFALDINO enters.

TRUFFALDINO: Later, eat later! How many times must I swallow the word "later" before I finally choke on my pride? How much more can I take? If I knew where my master was going to stay, I could beg a bite on credit... But no! My master leaves his bags on the dock, me on the street, and my stomach with nothing to feed on but anger. (holds his stomach) What? I know, my darling. If I could just find the smallest opportunity to make a few lira, then I can put some food into you... What?... Where! (stomach turns him around) I'll give him a try, my darling!

        (FLORINDO enters with PORTER)

FLORINDO: See that?

PORTER: Yes, sir.

FLORINDO: An inn.

PORTER: I know that, sir.

FLORINDO: Come on, come on!

PORTER: I've got to stop, sir.

FLORINDO: We stopped three times already.

PORTER: I beg you to understand, sir. Oh...it's falling, sir!

FLORINDO: I thought you porters had muscles?

PORTER: I'm not a porter, sir. I'm a waiter.

FLORINDO: A what?

TRUFFALDINO: (flexing his muscles and clearing his throat) Did
                I hear you say muscles, sir?

FLORINDO: (quickly turning) What? So I did. I haven't seen
                one since I arrived.

TRUFFALDINO: Now you do, sir. At your service. May I take that?
                Thank you. You wouldn't have another bag, sir? I·
                do have my left arm.

FLORINDO: No, no, that's all.

TRUFFALDINO: A master with so little?

FLORINDO: A master who travels light.

TRUFFALDINO: Oh...my favourite kind.

PORTER: Excuse me, sir?

FLORINDO: Yes?

PORTER: (extending his hand) For the work I've done. You
                haven't forgotten?

FLORINDO: What work?

PORTER: From the gondola to here, sir.

FLORINDO: Thirty yards.

PORTER: Thirty yards, sir.

FLORINDO: Go away!

PORTER: But, sir?

TRUFFALDINO: You heard the master. Go! Now!

PORTER:	Scab! (exits)
TRUFFALDINO:	How dare he? Are we ready, sir?
FLORINDO:	Yes, let's inspect this inn.
TRUFFALDINO:	Oh, I've already taken care of the preliminaries, sir
FLORINDO:	You have?
TRUFFALDINO:	Premonition, sir. I do use other muscles. Now they have a mezzo-mezzo stable. And the rooms... Well, what can I say. Too grand for a master's servant, sir... But for a master!
FLORINDO:	Are you working for this inn?
TRUFFALDINO:	Oh no, sir. I just knew you were coming. Come. Let's get you registered. The food is excellent.
FLORINDO:	Just a moment. Are you employed?
TRUFFALDINO:	(looks to audience and then back) At the moment, sir
FLORINDO:	Now.
TRUFFALDINO:	Here?
FLORINDO:	Yes! Here.
TRUFFALDINO:	(smiling) No. (to audience) It's just as easy to shrink the truth as it is to stretch it.
FLORINDO:	How would you like to work for me?
TRUFFALDINO:	(to audience) Can I let loyalty get in the way of hunger? (grabbing stomach) I won't! I won't, my darling.
FLORINDO:	What?
TRUFFALDINO:	I will! I will!
FLORINDO:	Good. How much?
TRUFFALDINO:	Well, my previous master...
FLORINDO:	This?
TRUFFALDINO:	Well...
FLORINDO:	That?

TRUFFALDINO:	Yes...that...but...
FLORINDO:	He didn't give you this much I'm sure?
TRUFFALDINO:	I'm sure he won't. I'll take it.
FLORINDO:	Not just yet. A test. I know your strength. I'd like to see your speed. There will be a tip.
TRUFFALDINO:	Check those feet, sir.
FLORINDO:	No complications.
TRUFFALDINO:	Quick, sir. (goes for the money)
FLORINDO:	Tips come after tasks. First take my trunk inside. Then to the post office. Ask for all the mail concerning Florindo Aretusi. Are you listening?
TRUFFALDINO:	(has been preoccupied with stomach) I'm trying, sir.
FLORINDO:	I'll need it immediately.
TRUFFALDINO:	Will you be eating, sir?
FLORINDO:	I will.
TRUFFALDINO:	And me?
FLORINDO:	If you like!
TRUFFALDINO:	I like! I like!
FLORINDO:	Then get to work. Oh, what's your name?
TRUFFALDINO:	Truffaldino Battachio.
FLORINDO:	Where are you from? Don't tell me Turin.
TRUFFALDINO:	No?
FLORINDO:	No.
TRUFFALDINO:	Then tell you what, sir?
FLORINDO:	Where you're from.
TRUFFALDINO:	You can't tell, sir?
FLORINDO:	No.
TRUFFALDINO:	Bergamo, sir.
FLORINDO:	Bergamo? Are they all like you?

TRUFFALDINO: They try to be, sir.

                    (FLORINDO exits)

Two salaries! Two masters! I dare not think of the
outcome. Oh well, where is that first one? Too
young to be a master anyway. Huh...I better go. I'll
need that tip. But if I'm not here. (looking at
stomach) Do you want me to be a servant to two? You
do? But if one finds out... I've got the other?
And if the other finds out... I've got the first!
Very good, my darling. Of course I can. I'll serve
two.

                    (BEATRICE and BRIGHELLA enter)

BEATRICE: What are you doing?

TRUFFALDINO: I was just on my way to fetch your trunk.

BEATRICE: Haven't you done that yet? I'll be in this inn
                here.

TRUFFALDINO: You're staying here?

BRIGHELLA: What tone of voice is that?

TRUFFALDINO: You're staying here?

BEATRICE: Of course I'm staying here. Now go! Get my trunks.
                Stop off at the post office. There will be letters
                waiting for me and my sister, Beatrice Rasponi. Did
                you hear that?

TRUFFALDINO: Will she be staying with you?

BRIGHELLA: Are you sure it's wise to have the letters sent to
                the both of you?

BEATRICE: My steward will be writing. He doesn't know to whom
                just yet. Off Truffaldino! Letters, my trunks, then
                back to me. I thought you were hungry?

TRUFFALDINO: Hungry?

BEATRICE: Then go! The sooner you're back the sooner you'll
                eat. I understand Signor Brighella is the finest
                of chefs.

TRUFFALDINO: It's a pleasure to meet you, sir.

BEATRICE: Come, Brighella. An appetizer while we wait for my
                news?

BRIGHELLA:	An excellent idea. There's a lovely white fish that's recently swum into the canal. (exits)
TRUFFALDINO:	White fish?!

(SILVIO enters)

SILVIO:	Hey! Hey! Where's your master?
TRUFFALDINO:	(long pause) My master?
SILVIO:	You don't know where your master is?
TRUFFALDINO:	Umm... I do, sir. (looks to audience and mouths "which one")
SILVIO:	Where?
TRUFFALDINO:	In there...
SILVIO:	Deliver a message.
TRUFFALDINO:	(aside) No respect. No respect.
SILVIO:	Tell him a man of honour is waiting for him outside.
TRUFFALDINO:	(aside) I never knew honour to be so nervous.
SILVIO:	Go! Hurry! Tell him I'm waiting.
FLORINDO:	Truffaldino! What are you doing?
TRUFFALDINO:	I'm just fetching your trunk, sir.
FLORINDO:	Who's that?
TRUFFALDINO:	That man wants to see my master, sir. Oh!
FLORINDO:	Really? I don't recognize him, Truffaldino. Why would he want to see me?
TRUFFALDINO:	It's Venice, sir. It's Venice. They're all the same here. Now I'll rush and fetch those letters for you. I was rudely interrupted. (exits)
FLORINDO:	Sir? Was it something I said? Sir! You asked to see me?
SILVIO:	No, I did not. I am waiting to see the cowardly master of that idiot servant.
FLORINDO:	That, sir, is my servant.

SILVIO: Your servant, sir?

FLORINDO: He is.

SILVIO: Oh. Are you sure?

FLORINDO: Of course I'm sure.

SILVIO: Well then he waits on two.

FLORINDO: Aren't you a bit presumptuous, sir?

SILVIO: Oh! I'm sorry, sir.

FLORINDO: Mistaken identity is not uncommon.

SILVIO: Will you please forgive me?

FLORINDO: I accept your apology.

SILVIO: Thank you, sir. Are you a visitor here?

FLORINDO: I am.

SILVIO: And where are you from if I may ask?

FLORINDO: Turin.

SILVIO: Turin? Have you all come as a group? You said
            Turin?

FLORINDO: Yes, Turin.

SILVIO: The man I need to see is also from Turin.

FLORINDO: You wouldn't know his name would you?

SILVIO: I know more than his name.

FLORINDO: You do?

SILVIO: To begin with, his name is Federigo Rasponi. Are
            you familiar with that one?

FLORINDO: Sadly...I think...I am. He's dead, sir. I hope.

SILVIO: Dead? I'd hardly call him dead. Just this morning
            he arrived from Turin to claim my fiancé as his.

FLORINDO: That's impossible, sir. Rasponi, I tell you, is
            dead!

SILVIO: So you say... Then he must have returned from the
            dead.

FLORINDO: Impossible.

SILVIO: I was saying the same thing myself. One moment dead.
              Another alive.

FLORINDO: Nonsense.

SILVIO: I tell you it's true. I saw him myself.

FLORINDO: Rasponi here?

SILVIO: Yes.

FLORINDO: Federigo Rasponi?

SILVIO: Federigo Rasponi!

FLORINDO: Here?

SILVIO: Yes. Here.

FLORINDO: It can't be!

SILVIO: Are you well, sir? May I be of some assistance to
              you? Let's begin with introductions. Start over.

FLORINDO: Yes. I wish that was possible.

SILVIO: Your name?

FLORINDO: Ummm.

SILVIO: You've forgotten your name, sir?

FLORINDO: No, no. My name? Right. I am Orazio Ardenti.

SILVIO: Silvio Lombardi!

FLORINDO: It's a pleasure to meet you.

SILVIO: I'm sure. If I can be of any assistance to you in
              any capacity, please call on me. Ciao, Orazio.

FLORINDO: And to you,sir. Thank you. Thank you.

                        (SILVIO exits)

              Rasponi here? I thought I killed him. My God,
              what's happened to my thrust?

                              (TRUFFALDINO enters with PORTER. PORTER
                              is carrying BEATRICE's trunk)

TRUFFALDINO: Do you know how many trunks I've carried in my day? (sees FLORINDO) Oh! Right. Go to the end of the street and wait there.

PORTER: But, sir?

TRUFFALDINO: Go!

FLORINDO: I've got to get back to Turin.

(PORTER exits)

TRUFFALDINO: (to FLORINDO) Quick enough, sir?

FLORINDO: To Turin!

TRUFFALDINO: To Turin? Now?

FLORINDO: Yes.

TRUFFALDINO: (to stomach) I know, my darling.

FLORINDO: What?

TRUFFALDINO: Before lunch, sir?

FLORINDO: No, no we'll have lunch. The letters?

TRUFFALDINO: Right here...sir...right...yes...somewhere...I know..

FLORINDO: I'm waiting, Truffaldino!

TRUFFALDINO: I'm looking as quickly as I can, sir.

FLORINDO: They're very important!

TRUFFALDINO: (searching frantically) Please, sir. I must tell you these letters are not all for you. A friend of mine, another servant, stopped me on the way to the post office and asked me to pick up his master's letters. I believe there's one here for you somewhere Yes. It must be one of these...

FLORINDO: Let me look for myself.

TRUFFALDINO: I'm sure you understand?

FLORINDO: What? (notices letters)

TRUFFALDINO: Servants helping servants. You know.

FLORINDO: "To Beatrice Rasponi of Venice"?!

TRUFFALDINO:	Oh, you found the one you need?
FLORINDO:	What is your friend's name?
TRUFFALDINO:	Oh, why it's...Pasquale, sir!
FLORINDO:	Do you know his master?
TRUFFALDINO:	I've never seen him, sir.
FLORINDO:	But if he sent you for these letters, he must have given you his name?
TRUFFALDINO:	(aside) To play dumb would be obvious. To be honest could be fatal. (to FLORINDO) Name, sir?
FLORINDO:	You don't remember his name?
TRUFFALDINO:	He wrote it down for me, sir. After it's use was fulfilled, I threw it away.
FLORINDO:	Where does this Pasquale live?
TRUFFALDINO:	We don't discuss accommodation, sir.
FLORINDO:	Then where are you to meet him?
TRUFFALDINO:	A rendezvous in the piazza, sir.
FLORINDO:	Can she be here?
TRUFFALDINO:	Will you please give me his letter, sir and I will go and find him.
FLORINDO:	No, I must examine this letter.
TRUFFALDINO:	Does examine mean open, sir?
FLORINDO:	It does.
TRUFFALDINO:	You've opened it, sir!
FLORINDO:	(reading aside) "Dear Signora Beatrice, the investigation about the death of your brother revealed that you have fled to Venice to be with your lover Florindo Aretusi. It is also known that you are wearing your dead brother's clothes. The Court of Justice has sent out a warrant for your arrest as an accomplice. This letter has been sent through two couriers so as not to reveal your present whereabouts. If there is anything more that you must know, I will send the information at once. Your humble servant, Antonio." Bless you, Antonio.

TRUFFALDINO: Sir! You read the entire letter.

FLORINDO: She's here! In her brother's clothes. This confirm.
                 the love her brother refused to see. I must find her
                 Truffaldino!

TRUFFALDINO: Yes, sir?

FLORINDO: Find this Pasquale. Find out who his master is and
                 bring him to me.

TRUFFALDINO: I will try, sir. But you must give me back his
                 letter so he can give it to the master you wish to
                 see, sir. Oh sir, the letter is open and if his
                 master finds out, there will certainly be a beating
                 for my dear friend Pasquale. You know how masters
                 can be, sir...

FLORINDO: Tell him it was sent like that.

TRUFFALDINO: Sir?

FLORINDO: What can he say? He knows you can't read.

TRUFFALDINO: You knew?

FLORINDO: Please do me this favour, Truffaldino. There will
                 be a reward for both you and Pasquale.

TRUFFALDINO: Thank you, but how soon will we be leaving for Turin,
                 sir?

FLORINDO: We're not going to Turin. Federigo in Venice.
                 Beatrice in Venice. I must find her first. Hurry!
                 Find Pasquale! (exits)

TRUFFALDINO: I still need to eat, sir! I tried my darling. I
                 tried. My young master will never accept an opened
                 letter. It must be sealed. But how am I going to do
                 it? (searches in his pocket, pulls out a piece of
                 bread) Ah, bread. This should seal it. My last
                 bit of nourishment. Let this be an investment
                 towards a larger meal! (to stomach) What can I do?
                 (puts bread in his mouth) Ohh...what a taste.
                 Slower. Slower. (swallows) Oh, what have you done?
                 Again! (tears off another piece of bread) Don't my
                 darling. Wait! Wait! (struggling, pulls it out of
                 his mouth) Restraint! There! (seals letter) Not
                 too bad. Creative. Oh! I've forgotten! Porter!
                 Porter!

PORTER: Please tell me where to put it.

TRUFFALDINO: Don't tempt me. Into the inn!

PORTER: By the way, I'm not a porter...I'm a waiter! (exits)

                    (BEATRICE enters)

BEATRICE: Is that my trunk, Truffaldino?

TRUFFALDINO: It is, sir. Isn't he doing well? You see I...

BEATRICE: Have you been to the post office?

TRUFFALDINO: I have.

BEATRICE: And?

TRUFFALDINO: Yes?

BEATRICE: Are there any letters for me?!

TRUFFALDINO: I'd say yes, sir.

BEATRICE: Well?!

TRUFFALDINO: There's one for your sister. None for you. I'm
                sorry, sir. You've got to learn to write back, sir.

BEATRICE: Where is my sister's letter?

TRUFFALDINO: Here, sir. All tucked away.

BEATRICE: Why, it's been opened!

TRUFFALDINO: Not opened, sir?

BEATRICE: It's been sealed with bread.

TRUFFALDINO: Bread, sir?

BEATRICE: Bread, sir.

TRUFFALDINO: A creative way of sealing, sir.

BEATRICE: I'll show you a creative way of...

TRUFFALDINO: Please, sir! I'm just your servant. Serving it as
                it is.

BEATRICE: Who else read this?

TRUFFALDINO: I shall choose not to hear that, sir. I am an
                honourable man and...

BEATRICE:	Are you sure about that?
TRUFFALDINO:	Whether I'm an honourable man or whether someone has read it?
BEATRICE:	I hope you're telling the truth, Truffaldino.
TRUFFALDINO:	Truth?
BEATRICE:	Thank God for Antonio. Now there is a faithful servant. Unpack my trunk and I'll return shortly. Then we can eat.
TRUFFALDINO:	Eat? Oh that's very kind of you, sir.
BEATRICE:	I just hope that no one...
TRUFFALDINO:	Has read that, sir?
BEATRICE:	Yes. Have you seen Signor Pantalone, Truffaldino?
TRUFFALDINO:	Uh, no sir. Signor Pantalone? Uhh no, sir.
BEATRICE:	I will need that money. (exits)
TRUFFALDINO:	What more can I expect from myself? I'm doing so well. I never expected this from me! (to stomach) I know, I know, my darling. I'll get you something. It's me. Truffaldino!

(PANTALONE enters)

PANTALONE:	Excuse me. Are you practising for something?
TRUFFALDINO:	Oh no, sir!
PANTALONE:	Where is your master?
TRUFFALDINO:	Umm...here, sir.
PANTALONE:	Ahh.
TRUFFALDINO:	Umm...not here, sir.
PANTALONE:	Oh?
TRUFFALDINO:	Will be here, sir.
PANTALONE:	Oh! Trust him? I will. I will. Well, when he returns, will you give this to him? Please be very careful.
TRUFFALDINO:	Yes, sir.

PANTALONE: I can't do it. (struggling with TRUFFALDINO)

TRUFFALDINO: Sir, you can trust me.

PANTALONE: I will! I will!

TRUFFALDINO: That was easy, sir.

PANTALONE: I did! I did!

TRUFFALDINO: Congratulations.

PANTALONE: Oh thank you! (exits)

TRUFFALDINO: You're welcome. (aside) Now to whom am I to give
                this?

FLORINDO: (enters) Where's Pasquale, Truffaldino?

TRUFFALDINO: Oh excuse me, sir. I haven't been able to find him,
                sir. But I may have found something else...depending..

FLORINDO: What is it?

TRUFFALDINO: Money, sir.

FLORINDO: Money?

TRUFFALDINO: Were you expecting this?

FLORINDO: I had contracted for some credit. Yes.

TRUFFALDINO: They do have good service here don't they, sir?

FLORINDO: No message? Just money?

TRUFFALDINO: Just "to give it to my master", sir.

FLORINDO: Well they are efficient. Well? Am I not your
                master?

TRUFFALDINO: Of course you are, sir. (gives him the money)

FLORINDO: You've got to find Pasquale!

TRUFFALDINO: I will, sir. But I don't think it's possible to put
                in a really thorough search until I'm able to eat
                something. (to stomach) I'm asking! I'm asking!

FLORINDO: Asking what?

TRUFFALDINO: My stomach, sir. You see she's been without.

FLORINDO: Your stomach?

TRUFFALDINO: Needs food, sir. Desperately!

FLORINDO: Why didn't you say something?

TRUFFALDINO: Say something, sir? Did I not? You're right, sir.
                Humble me. I work too hard.

FLORINDO: And I do appreciate it. I'll meet you in Brighella's
                dining room.

TRUFFALDINO: Yes sir!

FLORINDO: After you find Pasquale.

TRUFFALDINO: I will sir!

                        (FLORINDO exits)

                I will? (exits)

Act One, Scene Three

In the house of PANTALONE.

PANTALONE: Why don't you sit down, Clarice? Not now Smeraldina.

CLARICE: How can I, Papa?

SMERALDINA: Sir?

PANTALONE: Please. Trust me. I'm your father. I love you.
                Would I dare do anything to hurt my poor, poor
                Clarice?

CLARICE: You already have. And stop calling me your poor,
             poor Clarice. What other father would arrange a
             marriage for his daughter without either having seen
             the man?

PANTALONE: But you have seen him. (to SMERALDINA) Get out!

                    (SMERALDINA exits)

CLARICE: Don't be such a hypocrite, Papa!

PANTALONE: How dare you! Think of your poor mother.

CLARICE: My mother would not have consented to an agreement
             without a formal introduction.

PANTALONE: Introduction? The man has a reputation. Need we
             know any more?

CLARICE: Yes!

PANTALONE: What?

CLARICE: Need I say, Papa!

PANTALONE: I have completely explained myself to you, Clarice.
             I wouldn't be the man I am today if I had a trail of
             broken agreements behind me. You will marry Signor
             Rasponi. It is agreed upon!

CLARICE: But it is not my agreement. Somehow you have
             forgotten that.

PANTALONE: Sit down!

CLARICE: What?

PANTALONE: Sit down.

                    (CLARICE sits)

             Thank you.

CLARICE: Papa?! (rising)

PANTALONE: Please...let me...

                    (CLARICE sits)

             Thank you. (pause) What is the highest order of
             mercantilism? Reputation. A merchant can achieve
             no more than reputation in his lifetime. Do you know
             how I've dreamt to have a son take over my business?

PANTALONE: (cont'd)
Could I simply let it die? It's just as difficult for a father to find a husband for his daughter as it is for a merchant to find an heir to his business. Do you think a reputable merchant would recommend someone inferior to himself for his daughter? NO! There's a future to be thought of. Yours. And mine! And let the future be good business for the both of us.

(SMERALDINA enters)

SMERALDINA: Sir?

PANTALONE: You must believe me, Clarice. What is it, Smeraldina

SMERALDINA: Signor Rasponi is here to see you, sir.

PANTALONE: Tell the good man to come in.

CLARICE: I beg of you to reconsider, Papa?!

SMERALDINA: My lady's crying, sir!

PANTALONE: It's just happiness, Smeraldina. Although she doesn' know it just yet.

SMERALDINA: Before you weep too much madam, I would reconsider. He is a handsome man.

PANTALONE: Another plus, Clarice!

SMERALDINA: Almost too handsome.

PANTALONE: Not for my Clarice.

SMERALDINA: If it were me...

CLARICE: What?

SMERALDINA: Well, I would be laughing all the way to the altar.

PANTALONE: Go Smeraldina. Send him in.

(SMERALDINA exits)

Clarice? Can't you stop crying for one moment?

CLARICE: Can't you see I'm scared, Papa!

PANTALONE: There's nothing to be scared about. Do you realize the consequences if you don't fulfill the agreement?

CLARICE:	Your reputation?
PANTALONE:	That's my Clarice.

(BEATRICE enters)

BEATRICE:	Signor Pantalone?
PANTALONE:	Ahh, you have arrived. Tell me, did you receive my money? I left it with your servant.
BEATRICE:	No.
PANTALONE:	No?
BEATRICE:	Not to worry. My servant is a trustworthy man. I just haven't seen him. May I ask how your daughter is?
PANTALONE:	Oh well...she's overcome by it all. First your death, then another suitor, now you again. You can understand.
BEATRICE:	Signor Pantalone, would you do me the favour of leaving us alone?

(CLARICE immediately stands up)

PANTALONE:	It would be my pleasure. Sit down, Clarice. I'll just retreat out the door and... Smeraldina?! (exits)
BEATRICE:	If you'll allow me...
CLARICE:	Stand back! Away from me. I don't trust my feelings at close range, sir.
BEATRICE:	If you just give me a chance to prove to you who I really am.
CLARICE:	I know perfectly well who you are, sir. Very different from the man I love. Silvio Lombardi! Do you hear that name? That is the name I will always have in my heart every moment you and I are married. Do you have no compassion for love?
BEATRICE:	I do.
CLARICE:	You see how I am. Do you want a wife like that?
BEATRICE:	No.
CLARICE:	No?

BEATRICE: Look, you are not in love with me, are you?

CLARICE: No!

BEATRICE: Well?...

CLARICE: Yes?

BEATRICE: Ummm...

CLARICE: What?

BEATRICE: ...Can you keep a secret?

CLARICE: I want none of your little secrets, sir. Obviously I was one of your secrets and you didn't even care enough to include me in it.

BEATRICE: I too am in love with another.

CLARICE: No you're not!

BEATRICE: Yes I am.

CLARICE: But you're in love with me.

BEATRICE: No I'm not. Now, may I continue?

CLARICE: Don't try to trick me, sir.

BEATRICE: It won't be necessary.

CLARICE: We'll see.

BEATRICE: I am not Federigo Rasponi, madam.

CLARICE: Not Federigo?

BEATRICE: His sister Beatrice.

CLARICE: Do you expect me to believe that? A woman?!

BEATRICE: Yes...a woman.

CLARICE: I have been deceived further than I had thought I had What kind of an agreement do you have with my father?

BEATRICE: None. My brother is dead, Clarice.

CLARICE: Dead?!

BEATRICE: Killed by the hand of my own lover, Florindo Aretusi, the man I want to marry. The man I am searching for

BEATRICE:	(cont'd) disguised in my brother's clothes. God forgive me.
CLARICE:	Really?
BEATRICE:	Yes.
CLARICE:	I must tell Silvio!
BEATRICE:	I beg you not to.
CLARICE:	No?
BEATRICE:	Not for the moment.
CLARICE:	Why?
BEATRICE:	I need time, Clarice. Time to find Florindo. I know he's here in Venice. Please. Will you keep my secret?
CLARICE:	Of course.
BEATRICE:	Let's promise as women do in these most desperate moments, to help each other.
CLARICE:	As friends?
BEATRICE:	I'd like that.

(They embrace. PANTALONE enters)

PANTALONE:	(aside) Oh, I don't believe it! After all the worry I've been sweating over for days, it has been taken care of, in minutes. (to BEATRICE) Bravo Signor Federigo! You are a master, sir!
BEATRICE:	And you are perceptive, sir.
PANTALONE:	Why thank you, Signor Federigo. Someone has finally noticed.
CLARICE:	(to BEATRICE) Now what?
PANTALONE:	We must not lose the momentum of this moment. A wedding!
CLARICE:	Papa!
PANTALONE:	Soon!
CLARICE:	But, Papa...

PANTALONE: Tonight! You must trust me, Clarice. I know what's best for you and I know you know that too.

BEATRICE: Sir, I would like to complete our financial agreement before we begin making the arrangements for the wedding.

PANTALONE: No problem at all. Two hours will be enough.

BEATRICE
& CLARICE: But...

PANTALONE: Now I must go speak with Signor Silvio.

BEATRICE
& CLARICE: But...

PANTALONE: It is from my mouth, the mouth of a man of perception and reputation that he deserves to hear the news.

CLARICE: Papa?

PANTALONE: (impatient) Clarice?

CLARICE: Be gentle with him.

PANTALONE: I will, my dear.

CLARICE: He is passionate, Papa. He could do something rash!

PANTALONE: I know, I know. But what do you want? Two husbands? (laughs to himself) Well, he knew where he stood, didn't he? I was an honest man on this, wasn't I. I just hope nothing else goes wrong. Don't you?

CLARICE: Papa?

PANTALONE: Clarice.

CLARICE: Maybe I should tell him.

BEATRICE: No!

PANTALONE: Out of the question. One never really knows what passion will do. Good day to you both. At last!

> (PANTALONE exits with a laugh while BEATRICE and CLARICE stare at one another)

CLARICE: Don't you ever kiss me again.

Act One, Scene Four

Courtyard of PANTALONE's house. LOMBARDI
and SILVIO enter creeping.

LOMBARDI: (loud whisper) Silvio!

SILVIO: (loud whisper, he has been hiding around the corner
                of the house) Don't scare me like that! Father,
                please go.

LOMBARDI: What are you doing here?

SILVIO: Please, Father!

LOMBARDI: I have a right to know.

SILVIO: I'm going to confront Signor Pantalone.

LOMBARDI: Here? In front of his house? Are you a fool?

SILVIO: He's the fool, Father. Can't you see?

LOMBARDI: This ill humour of yours will never solve your
                problems.

SILVIO: And who is the cause of my ill humour?

LOMBARDI: Two fools fighting with each other will never discover
                the truth. Then again... Of course... Let me talk
                with him. Let me see if reason is within his scope.
                I am not only your father but I am also the right man
                in this case. Calm, dutiful and capable of bringing
                men's minds to rational thought. Now go! I'll wait
                here for Signor Pantalone.

SILVIO: But Father, it is my problem and I must deal with it
                in the fashion I am best suited for. (pulling out
                his sword)

LOMBARDI: That is not your best fashion, Silvio. Go!

SILVIO: You'll speak to him?

LOMBARDI: Didn't I just say I would?

SILVIO: Thank you, Father. (exits)

LOMBARDI: Oh, my poor son. Caught between the ghost of a dead
              man and the father of a lost bride. What a nightmare!
              I've got to control myself. Grip. Grip your anger
              Lombardi.

                         (PANTALONE enters)

PANTALONE: (noticing LOMBARDI) Ahh!

LOMBARDI: Signor Pantalone?

PANTALONE: Dr. Lombardi! What a coincidence. I was just looking
              for you and your son.

LOMBARDI: (aside) A jovial mood. Perhaps he's reconsidered.
              (to PANTALONE) You've changed your mind. Ahh, good
              for you! I knew we could count on you, Signor
              Pantalone. I was just telling my son that your
              irrational behaviour was only the sign of a devoted
              father.

PANTALONE: Irrational? Devoted?

LOMBARDI: Aren't you?

PANTALONE: Absolutely. I must act as a father should.

LOMBARDI: Now there you are. Coming back to life. To your
              real self.

PANTALONE: Oh, I never thought I lost him.

LOMBARDI: Only for a moment, sir. We realized you'd come to
              your senses.

PANTALONE: Senses, hell! It was a sense of logic.

LOMBARDI: An agreement?

PANTALONE: Created and signed in an honest manner.

LOMBARDI: And then you realized...that you were... (waiting
              for PANTALONE to respond) Well sir, no apologies
              are needed among old friends.

PANTALONE: Always realized that, Lombardi.

LOMBARDI: Of course. Families, sir. And besides, where do your daughter's sympathies really lie anyway?

PANTALONE: Yes. I know that now. I'm glad I've made the proper decision. She seems so content that I can't really let her down, can I?

LOMBARDI: Oh bless your heart. You are a kind and gentle soul.

PANTALONE: I hope so, Lombardi.

LOMBARDI: Well, my son will surely be pleased.

PANTALONE: You give him that much credit?

LOMBARDI: Wouldn't you?

PANTALONE: Well, it would call for a strong man considering how much he's invested.

LOMBARDI: He'll be a good husband, sir.

PANTALONE: I'm sure.

LOMBARDI: And an even better son-in-law.

PANTALONE: Yes. Just a moment here, Lombardi?...

LOMBARDI: I know. Father to father. My dear wife, bless her, would have loved a daughter.

PANTALONE: I beg of you, sir. Let me speak more than just one word here.

LOMBARDI: Do. Do. I'm just so relieved.

PANTALONE: I'm not so sure.

LOMBARDI: Oh, don't let my usual ways deceive you. I am ecstatic!

PANTALONE: I'd wait before removing your disguise, sir.

LOMBARDI: I beg your pardon?

PANTALONE: I've been trying to tell you that...

LOMBARDI: What?

PANTALONE: Well...

LOMBARDI: Don't tell me...

PANTALONE: Yes. Not my fault, sir.

LOMBARDI: Oh, I can't stand it. (to audience) I've given
              myself away. To hell with you. To hell with your
              daughter. Here an agreement. There an agreement.
              You are not the man you think you are. Dishonest and
              unethical. Vivat post funera vertis.

PANTALONE: How dare you!

LOMBARDI: (exasperated, mimicking) Your daughter seems so
              content.

PANTALONE: She is, sir.

LOMBARDI: At first I agreed with my son. The contract was
              sealed between himself and your daughter. But now,
              given the type of family she comes from and her
              vulnerability to such mad behaviour, perhaps it would
              be safer for us to think otherwise.

PANTALONE: Go ahead! It would be easier for us all!

LOMBARDI: You may still pay for this dishonour, sir. You have
              threatened our family. Omnia tempaes habent.

PANTALONE: Get out of my way.

LOMBARDI: Do you know our family?

PANTALONE: Never heard of them. I own this street. It is mine.
              Get off it now! Do you hear me?

LOMBARDI: (calmly to audience) Oh look at the raving gentleman
              ladies. Once we thought an honest merchant and father
              Poor Signor Pantalone.

PANTALONE: GET OUT!

LOMBARDI: Bonds, Signor Pantalone. It'll be the death of you.
              Beware ladies. Merchants and fathers. Fathers and
              merchants. One and the same. Hic fenis pandi.
              (exits)

PANTALONE: I beg of you, don't believe him. He's the fool! I'm
              a father first. Well...merchant too. Oh here comes
              the other half.

                      (SILVIO enters staring at PANTALONE)

              What is it? What is it?

SILVIO: My father tells me...

PANTALONE: Yes! Yes! It's all done. Clarice is content and
              the marriage shall take place.

SILVIO: You stand there and tell me that?

PANTALONE: Yes, I am standing here and telling you that.

SILVIO: You will ruin your reputation with this action.

PANTALONE: Never! It's good business.

SILVIO: There is not an ounce of a gentleman in you!

PANTALONE: Do you know to whom you speak?!

SILVIO: You tempt me, sir.

PANTALONE: Oh, I shouldn't have asked. Forget it.

SILVIO: You scoundrel! Low, cheap, ruinous...

PANTALONE: I am your elder.

SILVIO: And closer, therefore, to the grave!

PANTALONE: Now don't you threaten me!

SILVIO: In public view I will have you on your knees in less
              than...

PANTALONE: Dare you draw your sword?

SILVIO: Easily done, sir.

PANTALONE: What? Is he going to do it?

SILVIO: Now!

PANTALONE: Murder! Murder!

                        (Stepping in front of PANTALONE, BEATRICE
                        enters, sword drawn)

BEATRICE: Stand back Signor Pantalone!

PANTALONE: Signor Federigo! I need help!

SILVIO: Just the man I'm looking for.

BEATRICE: May I help you, sir? (aside) What have I done?

PANTALONE: (creeping away)   I'll just go inside if you don't mind. (exits)

SILVIO: You may help me, sir, by standing ready.

BEATRICE: Duels should be fought rationally, sir.

SILVIO: No time for that, you frozen Turinese!

BEATRICE: Why you... (begins to fence) Speak to me Venetian! Speak to me!

(SILVIO retreats)

SILVIO: Father! Father!

BEATRICE: (pinning him down) No use calling for him, sir.

CLARICE: Please stop! Stop! Don't kill him!

BEATRICE: For you, my dear madam, I will spare this young fool.

CLARICE: (to SILVIO) Are you all right? No blood! No injury!

SILVIO: No blood? No injury?

BEATRICE: Now if you'll excuse me.

SILVIO: Traitor!

CLARICE: I love you! You've misunderstood!

SILVIO: I've misunderstood nothing!

BEATRICE: I'll just go. (exits)

CLARICE: I am truly yours.

SILVIO: Mine? Never!

CLARICE: Silvio?!

SILVIO: I hear you are content!

CLARICE: Only with you, Silvio.

SILVIO: Then why did your father say otherwise?

CLARICE: Oh...umm...I can't tell you just yet.

SILVIO: Deception! Deception! That's all your family knows.

CLARICE: I am sworn to secrecy.

SILVIO: And with whom is this faithful secret shared?

CLARICE: With whom? Oh, Silvio. With Signor Federigo.

SILVIO: You dare mention that name to me?

CLARICE: Didn't I prove my love by saving your life?

SILVIO: What life?

CLARICE: Oh, Silvio. I love you so much.

SILVIO: Hate would only give you a glimmer of what I feel now.

CLARICE: Then you want proof?

SILVIO: I can only believe your unfaithfulness.

CLARICE: Must I die before you believe me?

SILVIO: If that's your penalty.

CLARICE: Then you want me dead?

SILVIO: I do not know what I want.

CLARICE: Well, then. Here's proof. Oh Silvio! Oh Silvio!

                    (SMERALDINA enters)

SMERALDINA: Stop! What is this child's play? Love is surely
            easier than that, madam. I don't know about him.
            You might have thought this one out a little longer.
            How dare you push my lady that close to death?
            (throws down SILVIO's sword)

CLARICE: Nothing! You say nothing? You would have just stood
            there while I plunged your faithful sword into my
            heart? Would you have enjoyed wading in my blood?
            You probably would have run away to your father. You
            coward! You'll regret this. You're just... (starts
            to cry) I...I can't stand you! I hate you... (goes
            to him, stops herself, exits)

SMERALDINA: (to herself) If I asked what he was thinking I'd
            worry he might say nothing.

SILVIO: You believe that behaviour?

SMERALDINA: What?

SILVIO: That ludicrous threat of puncturing her heart?

SMERALDINA: If I had not arrived in time, sir...

SILVIO:	Such good timing, madam. Previously arranged surely?
SMERALDINA:	Arranged? What would have happened if I hadn't arrived?
SILVIO:	She would have killed herself.
SMERALDINA:	I'm not going to listen to this.
SILVIO:	Nonsense. That's all it was. Such sacrifice.
SMERALDINA:	And what sacrifices have you ever made, sir?
SILVIO:	Why I've... Why I've...
SMERALDINA:	Any with such devotion?
SILVIO:	Oh why, just the other day...
SMERALDINA:	Any with such commitment?! When have you ever stood your ground with your feelings, sir?
SILVIO:	But she was a faithless traitor! Nothing more!
SMERALDINA:	How predictable.
SILVIO:	Her being a traitor?
SMERALDINA:	No. You believing she was unfaithful.
SILVIO:	But she's going to marry that Rasponi!
SMERALDINA:	Not of her own doing, sir.
SILVIO:	Do you know her secret?
SMERALDINA:	No. Do you?
SILVIO:	No. I don't.
SMERALDINA:	So, just because she has a secret that makes her unfaithful.
SILVIO:	Well no...but...
SMERALDINA:	Just because she shares a secret?
SILVIO:	With Rasponi!
SMERALDINA:	Oh! And that makes her unfaithful.
SILVIO:	Of course!

SMERALDINA: Oh you men are so blind.

SILVIO: Blind? Who ever heard of such hypocrisy? Oh what
               am I talking to a servant for? I still must avenge
               the man who made her unfaithful. He shall die and
               Clarice will see what a fool she really was. (exits)

SMERALDINA: There's no use trying to make things clearer, it
               would only be more difficult for them. Poor men.
               (exits)

Act One, Scene Five

               BRIGHELLA'a inn. Two dining areas and
               a courtyard.

TRUFFALDINO: (backing out of the door) I was simply inspecting
               the kitchen.

NICKI: Oh, you were, were you?

TRUFFALDINO: My master has very specific tastes!

VITTORIO: Then what were you doing crawling around on the floor?

TRUFFALDINO: Checking the sanitary conditions!

NICKI: With a leg of lamb in your mouth?!

TRUFFALDINO: A little rare if you ask me!

VITTORIO: We were not asking you!

TRUFFALDINO: Obviously!

NICKI: Give that to me, servant!

TRUFFALDINO: I beg your pardon?

VITTORIO: If Master Brighella ever finds out.

TRUFFALDINO: I'm sure he would appreciate my concern.

NICKI: I'm sure he would.

(NICKI and VITTORIO exit)

TRUFFALDINO: You can't say I didn't try, my darling!

(FLORINDO enters)

FLORINDO: Is that you, Truffaldino?

TRUFFALDINO: Yes it is, sir.

FLORINDO: Have you found him yet?

TRUFFALDINO: I'm afraid not, sir. Lunch? May I ask where you are
                 going, sir?

FLORINDO: To the post office. They must know something.

TRUFFALDINO: But...

FLORINDO: (whistles) Oh! Gondola! (exits)

BEATRICE: (enters) Oh Truffaldino! Truffaldino?

TRUFFALDINO: I'm just dizzy. That's all. I'm fine.

BEATRICE: Where's the money Signor Pantalone gave you?

TRUFFALDINO: Signor Pantalone?... Ummm...yes sir, he did...give...
                 me...some...money.

BEATRICE: Where is it?

TRUFFALDINO: I umm...had to pay your bills.

BEATRICE: Bills?

TRUFFALDINO: The porter, the room and the gondola.

BEATRICE: Oh! Good thinking, Truffaldino.

TRUFFALDINO: Necessary when dealing with money, sir.

BEATRICE: No change?

TRUFFALDINO: It's Venice, sir.

BEATRICE: Oh well! Signor Pantalone will be joining me very shortly. We'll need a meal.

TRUFFALDINO: We couldn't agree with you more.

BEATRICE: Something special for my future father-in-law.

TRUFFALDINO: Would you like me to arrange it for you, sir?

BEATRICE: Thank you. And don't forget the wine, we'll need it.

TRUFFALDINO: Yes sir! Yes sir! Now's my chance to prove my real self. You see, my dream is to have an inn of my own some day. Oh, I know it sounds stupid. A servant with an inn. But I'm learning the trade. Do you think I'm the type to be a servant the rest of my life? Shut up, my darling. So now I'll prove what I've been learning. First lesson: decent bed. Second lesson: good meal. He'll see...they'll see... and maybe he...they will invest in me. Master Brighella! It is I, Truffaldino! Chef of Bergamo!

BRIGHELLA: What is it, Truffaldino?

TRUFFALDINO: Oh excuse me, sir. A meal for my master and Signor Pantalone. Is that possible?

BRIGHELLA: What do you mean is that possible? Just tell me what they want.

TRUFFALDINO: Well it's hard to know what's best in Venice, sir.

BRIGHELLA: So, we'll start with an antipasto misto.

TRUFFALDINO: You've got the squid?

BRIGHELLA: I won't answer that. Then maybe a minestrone?

TRUFFALDINO: Not with the antipasto, sir.

BRIGHELLA: You're telling me?!

TRUFFALDINO: Do you have a nice broth?

BRIGHELLA: First, how many dishes do they want?

TRUFFALDINO: Five or six.

BRIGHELLA: So now we got a pasta, no?

TRUFFALDINO: No.

BRIGHELLA: No?

TRUFFALDINO: No. Antipasto and broth. Nothing else.

BRIGHELLA: All right. A green pasta!

TRUFFALDINO: Do you have tagliarini?

BRIGHELLA: I do.

TRUFFALDINO: I'll take it. Veal?

BRIGHELLA: Rolled?

TRUFFALDINO: Perfect.

BRIGHELLA: Pig?

TRUFFALDINO: Are you going to have zabaglione?

BRIGHELLA: I could.

TRUFFALDINO: Then we'll take the pig. It'll coat the fat. How
               about a salad?

BRIGHELLA: Simple.

TRUFFALDINO: I'd like to keep it simple.

BRIGHELLA: That's what I mean!

TRUFFALDINO: Amaretto.

BRIGHELLA: Not with the meal.

TRUFFALDINO: After! After! Valpolicella...

BRIGHELLA: Well...

TRUFFALDINO: You've got a chianti?

BRIGHELLA: I could...

TRUFFALDINO: Cool.

BRIGHELLA: Damp.

TRUFFALDINO: Two bottles. All done. So who's going to do the
               tables, Signor Brighella?

BRIGHELLA: I've got two waiters, Truffaldino.

TRUFFALDINO: They're impossible.

BRIGHELLA: I'm telling you...

TRUFFALDINO: Me.

BRIGHELLA: You?

TRUFFALDINO: Setting the table is the most important. Like a good map. Telling you where you need to go next without thinking about it. It's got to be simple but complete enough to take you through. Enjoyably, that is. Enjoyably.

BRIGHELLA: I've been setting tables for twenty years! Look, say you got five to six dishes? Soup here. Antipasto there. Pasta there and kissing it will be the pig. Now the veal...

TRUFFALDINO: Kissing it, sir?

BRIGHELLA: It's a business term.

TRUFFALDINO: Oh I see. But, sir. If this is kissing that, then I don't understand why you separated these two since they've just got to know each other.

BRIGHELLA: But they're just the staples!

TRUFFALDINO: That's what I mean. It would be heartbreaking!

BRIGHELLA: All right! So we move that there.

TRUFFALDINO: That could be adultery, sir. Here, let me show you.

                  (BEATRICE enters with PANTALONE)

BEATRICE: Brighella? Is our meal ready?

BRIGHELLA: Oh sir, it will be. Just give me a moment. Nicki! Vittorio! (exits)

BEATRICE: I hope he won't disappoint us.

PANTALONE: One can't be too careful with Brighella's cuisine.

BEATRICE: Thank you for the advance...

PANTALONE: Oh? Oh! You got it?

BEATRICE: Yes and I was wondering if...

                  (BRIGHELLA enters)

BRIGHELLA: Would you like to sit over here while I create your meal? It's very comfortable. From my own vineyard, sirs. Many's the night my late but

BRIGHELLA:	(cont'd) demented wife...
PANTALONE:	Thank you, Brighella.
BRIGHELLA:	Prego. Truffaldino come.
BEATRICE:	Truffaldino?
TRUFFALDINO:	I'll take full responsibility, sir.
BEATRICE:	Thank you, Truffaldino.
TRUFFALDINO:	My pleasure. (exits)
PANTALONE:	I want to thank you for your hospitality, sir. And I am so pleased that you are sensitive to the activities going on in my dear little home. Bless its heart. Oh and by the way, thank you so much for saving my life from that rambunctious cadet!
BEATRICE:	It was nothing.
PANTALONE:	If only there was something I could do for you. Oh! Of course!
BEATRICE:	Yes?
PANTALONE:	What size are you?
BEATRICE:	Oh, well I...
PANTALONE:	Don't say no until you have seen it. A Florentine brocade. An original Laselva. It's one of the finest suits made in Italy. I was married in it.
BEATRICE:	Well, actually I was thinking...
TRUFFALDINO:	Whenever you are ready, gentlemen.
BEATRICE:	Thank you, Truffaldino.
PANTALONE:	You'll think about it?
BEATRICE:	I will.
TRUFFALDINO:	Come. Let me show you to your table. Its size will embrace your meal. A little in, sir. Oh, let me help you, sir. The pinch in will be that much more comfortable.

(PANTALONE yells)

BEATRICE:	Truffaldino!
PANTALONE:	First he confuses me. Then he amuses me. Now he irritates me.
BEATRICE:	Truffaldino, will you bring our food?
TRUFFALDINO:	My pleasure, sir. I'll just be a negotiation away. (sees VITTORIO carrying antipasto) One moment please. Nothing is served without my inspection. Now just hold it up here. Good. A little higher. Mmmm. Yes, yes... Anchovies? Not what I would have chosen but anchovies they are, I guess.
VITTORIO:	What are you doing?
BEATRICE:	(returning) Is that for us?

> (TRUFFALDINO is now holding the large plate of antipasto up to his nose)

TRUFFALDINO:	Yes sir, it is.
BEATRICE:	Well then, serve it. We're looking forward to it. (exits)
TRUFFALDINO:	(aside) So were you?... I'm sorry, my darling. (tries the antipasto) Get in there.

> (VITTORIO takes the antipasto in. NICKI enters)

NICKI:	Signor Brighella!
BRIGHELLA:	(off) What is it? (crash from the kitchen) Oh mama mia!
NICKI:	I thought you told me there was going to be a special waiter for this party!
TRUFFALDINO:	Here I am. No need to shout.
NICKI:	You?
TRUFFALDINO:	Aren't you a bit early with that?
NICKI:	Early? The soup is ready.
TRUFFALDINO:	Soup? Who bathed in this?
NICKI:	Are you going to take it or am I going to return it to the kitchen?

TRUFFALDINO: I'll take it. (takes it)

NICKI: Thank you. Are they through with the antipasto yet?

TRUFFALDINO: They've just started.

NICKI: Where are you from?

TRUFFALDINO: Bergamo.

NICKI: I might have known. (exits)

                    (FLORINDO enters)

FLORINDO: Truffaldino!

TRUFFALDINO: Sir! Are you all right?

FLORINDO: Barely. Oh Beatrice! Why aren't you looking for
               Pasquale?

TRUFFALDINO: (holding soup) May I suggest a little nourishment,
               sir?

FLORINDO: What have you been doing?

TRUFFALDINO: Preparing for your return, sir.

FLORINDO: You're so considerate, Truffaldino.

TRUFFALDINO: Oh thank you, sir. (aside) He seems to be the
               only one that notices.

FLORINDO: Is the table set?

TRUFFALDINO: Umm...not just yet, sir.

FLORINDO: But the soup seems to be ready.

TRUFFALDINO: It's a rustic setting, sir. Conducive to this hearty
               broth.

FLORINDO: Well bring it in. I couldn't do any worse than I'm
               doing so far.

TRUFFALDINO: I hope so, sir.

FLORINDO: What?

TRUFFALDINO: Right in there, sir.

FLORINDO: Thank you, Truffaldino. (exits into room)

TRUFFALDINO: You're welcome, sir. Now where was I going with this?

NICKI: (enters with veal) What have you been doing? We're getting backed up here.

TRUFFALDINO: Well I...

NICKI: Haven't you served that yet?

BEATRICE: (off) Our soup, Truffaldino! Our soup!

TRUFFALDINO: Yes sir! Please do me a favour?

NICKI: What about the scallopini?

TRUFFALDINO: Who?

NICKI: The veal.

TRUFFALDINO: I'll take it! But I want you to go in there and set the table for my master.

NICKI: Have they separated?

TRUFFALDINO: No. Just another. Shut up! Set it according to the same specifications as the other.

NICKI: As you wish. (exits)

TRUFFALDINO: One soup.

FLORINDO: Truffaldino!

TRUFFALDINO: Coming up!

                         (VITTORIO enters)

                 According to my specifications? (no response) How the table is set! How the table is set!

VITTORIO: I've got one goblet, one plate, one person. It won't be difficult.

TRUFFALDINO: Are you being flip?

FLORINDO: (off) Truffaldino!

TRUFFALDINO: Yes sir. I'll be right with you, sir! Get in there! Trumpets! Percussion! A little rapidmente!

                 (VITTORIO slowly exits, NICKI enters)

TRUFFALDINO: What is that?

NICKI: It's pasta, sir.

TRUFFALDINO: Is it mouldy?

NICKI: No!

TRUFFALDINO: Why is it so green?

NICKI: It's tagliarini.

TRUFFALDINO: Of course it is!

NICKI: This may be my last day here.

BEATRICE: The soup is cold, Truffaldino!

TRUFFALDINO: It's Spanish.

FLORINDO: The pasta's mouldy.

TRUFFALDINO: No it's not.

FLORINDO: Why is it so green?

TRUFFALDINO: It's tagliarini, sir.

FLORINDO: That's Spanish?

TRUFFALDINO: Si, sir!

FLORINDO: No, I don't.

                    (VITTORIO enters)

VITTORIO: I've forgotten!

TRUFFALDINO: Ummm, now let's see...

VITTORIO: Quickly, it's hot.

TRUFFALDINO: Yes. Hot.

BEATRICE: (off) Truffaldino!

VITTORIO: I can't wait much longer!

FLORINDO: (off) Truffaldino!

VITTORIO: You've got to make a decision.

TRUFFALDINO: Yes.

VITTORIO: Yes, what?

TRUFFALDINO: Give it to me.

VITTORIO: My pleasure. (exits)

TRUFFALDINO: Ow! Whose idea was this anyway? Of course, my
                 darling, I love serving two masters. Where is this
                 soup going anyway?

                         (NICKI enters)

NICKI: Excuse me.

TRUFFALDINO: What!

NICKI: I'll take that!

TRUFFALDINO: Where will you go with it?

NICKI: In here.

TRUFFALDINO: Are you sure?

NICKI: Of course I'm sure.

FLORINDO: (off) Pasta before soup, Truffaldino? What kind
                 of place is this?

TRUFFALDINO: Venetian!

                         (VITTORIO enters)

VITTORIO: Pig if you don't mind, sir.

TRUFFALDINO: Of course I don't mind. (notices it) Oh!

VITTORIO: What is it?

TRUFFALDINO: I think it's love.

VITTORIO: I think that's illegal!

                         (NICKI enters)

NICKI: Here's the cheese, sir.

TRUFFALDINO: (re-entering) Cheese? Now? I just served them
                 the pig.

NICKI: I believe there's been a mistake.

TRUFFALDINO: You mean that wasn't a pig?

NICKI:	Oh well, here's the cheese.
TRUFFALDINO:	Oh, then let's divide it.
NICKI:	As you wish.
TRUFFALDINO:	You take this half in there and I'll take the other.
NICKI:	But?
TRUFFALDINO:	I'm trying to be fair.
NICKI:	As you wish. (takes it to BEATRICE)
FLORINDO:	(off) Cheese?!
BEATRICE:	(off) Cheese?!
TRUFFALDINO:	Yes!
NICKI:	This is my last day! (exits)
VITTORIO:	Pig, sir?
TRUFFALDINO:	I think I'm in love again.
VITTORIO:	That could be pigamy!

                    (TRUFFALDINO looks to audience)

BEATRICE:	(off) Truffaldino!
FLORINDO:	(off) Truffaldino!
TRUFFALDINO:	Coming! A waiter's work is never done! Don't move. I love your ears.
BEATRICE:	(off) This is too cold and there's no gravy!
TRUFFALDINO:	Have you two met? Oh, you have? Maybe you can clear up something for me. What's going on in the kitchen? Take this one back in. Tell them it's cured and the gravy's optional . Oh, did you want to go? I wish you two would make up your mind. Take this one back in.
NICKI:	I'm not a waiter -- I'm a porter! (exits)
TRUFFALDINO:	You're a door knob! Now what am I going to do with these. Might as well.

                    (VITTORIO returns with soup)

VITTORIO: Sir? The soup... Hey!

TRUFFALDINO: I'm sorry. I couldn't help it. I'm starving.

VITTORIO: I'd say so judging by your eating habits.

TRUFFALDINO: Nothing wrong with a starving man's habits.

                          (BEATRICE enters)

BEATRICE: Truffaldino, what's going on out here? Is this a way
                 a servant serves his master?

TRUFFALDINO: Just tasting. For your own safety, sir.

BEATRICE: Not good enough. Hurry! So where are the grapes?
                 And no dessert?

TRUFFALDINO: I heard zabaglione, sir.

BEATRICE: Zabaglione with pig! We'd have to sweat it out for
                 a week! (exits)

TRUFFALDINO: Dessert! Dessert!

                          (BRIGHELLA enters)

BRIGHELLA: Here it is. My own creation. First time. Careful
                 please. They're extremely delicate.

TRUFFALDINO.   What are they?

BRIGHELLA: It's my own zabaglione. Aren't they lovely?
                 (exits)

TRUFFALDINO: Could we do something with these?

VITTORIO: I don't know. Whose are they?

                          (NICKI enters with grapes)

NICKI: I'm sorry, sir. You'll have to keep to your room.
                 This is a cross path.

FLORINDO: (drunk) Have you seen Beatrice?... A lovely girl
                 about this high?...

NICKI: May I suggest your room?

FLORINDO: Oh really? I didn't see her in there...

NICKI: Sir?

FLORINDO: Ohh...

                (NICKI waves him into his room, both exit.
                TRUFFALDINO enters)

TRUFFALDINO: (licking fingers) Not a bad dessert... I told
                them it was a Venetian sundae. Something warm from
                the canals. I think they'll enjoy it now. Now
                it's my turn.

                (VITTORIO enters with a bottle and glasses)

TRUFFALDINO: What is it you are carrying there?

VITTORIO: I won't allow you to drink this, sir.

TRUFFALDINO: You won't? All right, my darling. (he takes the
                bottle and drinks from it)

VITTORIO: But?

TRUFFALDINO: (takes another swig) Not bad. (to stomach) Not
                good?

                (NICKI enters, goes towards FLORINDO's
                room)

                I'll take those grapes. (voraciously eating) Oh
                my darling! Can you taste that? I know, my
                darling. Isn't it marvellous!

                        End Of Act One

Act Two, Scene One

Street in front of BRIGHELLA's inn.

SMERALDINA: You know what it's like to work for someone who is
               insanely overwrought? Well I do. My mistress is so
               dizzy with love that she will drive herself to death
               for one lover and send me carrying secret notes to
               the other. He's staying here. I know what goes on
               inside taverns. I can just imagine what's going on
               in there. Uh, oh. Now, now Smeraldina. What is
               it you are saying? Just what I'm feeling. So,
               what am I feeling then? (knocks on the door)

VITTORIO: (appears at door exhausted) Yes, madam?

SMERALDINA: (seeing VITTORIO is exhausted) Oh!... Ummm...

VITTORIO: What is it, madam? We're all exhausted in here.

SMERALDINA: Exhausted?

VITTORIO: Yes.

SMERALDINA: Is...is Signor Federigo Rasponi inside?

VITTORIO: Yes. He's here. A third of the reason I'm so
               exhausted. I think he's finished.

SMERALDINA: Finished?

VITTORIO: I'd say he was satisfied.

SMERALDINA: Satisfied?

VITTORIO: Why don't you come inside?

SMERALDINA: Me?

VITTORIO: You want me to ask him to come out?

SMERALDINA: Well I don't know. What condition is he in?

VITTORIO: Considering he's with Signor Pantalone now...

SMERALDINA: Really? Of course. A widower. Wouldn't you know it.

VITTORIO: Would you like to see his servant?

SMERALDINA: I am his servant. Oh...you mean Signor Federigo's? Oh well, yes I would. Or is he exhausted too?

VITTORIO: Well, I'd say he's had enough.

SMERALDINA: Had enough has he? We'll see.

                         (VITTORIO exits. SMERALDINA hums a
                         passionate song. TRUFFALDINO enters with
                         a hand towel, a bottle of wine and one
                         glass)

TRUFFALDINO: Who would dare interrupt my Amaretto?

SMERALDINA: Oh I'm sorry. It is I, Smeraldina.

TRUFFALDINO: Smeraldina. Oh, you should dare more often, my darling. (to stomach) Excuse me, my darling.

SMERALDINA: Oh sir... (aside) So forward.

TRUFFALDINO: Yes, madam?

SMERALDINA: (aside) Now so formal. My mistress has sent me with a message to your master.

TRUFFALDINO: And you want me to deliver it?

SMERALDINA: I do. I mean yes!

TRUFFALDINO: Is that all?

SMERALDINA: (aside) And I thought he had enough. (to TRUFFALDINO) Yes.

TRUFFALDINO: Oh. (aside) Surely she wants more.

SMERALDINA: Well... (spotting the Amaretto) perhaps?

TRUFFALDINO: Yes?

SMERALDINA: We could...

TRUFFALDINO: Yes?

SMERALDINA: Well...we might...

TRUFFALDINO: (thinking it's something else she wants) Of course.

SMERALDINA: Oh well then.

TRUFFALDINO: Where? When?

SMERALDINA: Here?

TRUFFALDINO: You're kidding?

SMERALDINA: Where else?

TRUFFALDINO: Where else? (aside) Have I got adventure on my hands?

SMERALDINA: (goes for the glass as TRUFFALDINO turns to the audience) Shall we?

TRUFFALDINO: (aside) And risk everything? (to SMERALDINA) You mean it?

SMERALDINA: Now...

TRUFFALDINO: Now?!

SMERALDINA: I'm sorry.

TRUFFALDINO: Don't be sorry!

SMERALDINA: Well it is your Amaretto.

TRUFFALDINO: What? Oh! Oh, of course. (aside) Do I feel like an idiot?

SMERALDINA: (as if she's about to toast) To...what?

TRUFFALDINO: To you!

SMERALDINA: Oh, why that's very kind of you.

TRUFFALDINO: (aside) She's driving me crazy!

SMERALDINA: And you too.

TRUFFALDINO: Me too?

SMERALDINA: Such good taste.

TRUFFALDINO: Recently acquired.

SMERALDINA: Oh, how long have you been working for this master?

TRUFFALDINO: Ummmm...

SMERALDINA: That long, eh?

TRUFFALDINO: Yes.

SMERALDINA: Me too.

TRUFFALDINO: Oh. Tell me, is your family...

SMERALINDA: Servants.

TRUFFALDINO: Mine too.

SMERALDINA: Who do they work for?

TRUFFALDINO: Oh, you wouldn't know them.

SMERALDINA: Bergamo?

TRUFFALDINO: Bergamo.

SMERALDINA: Could it be the Catatoni's?

TRUFFALDINO: What? Yes! How did you know?

SMERALDINA: Only family in Bergamo worth working for. Or
                that's what I hear.

TRUFFALDINO: If you're not working for them.

SMERALDINA: Batt...o...chio?

TRUFFALDINO: That's me.

SMERALDINA: Very famous mother and father.

TRUFFALDINO: It's true. I can't believe this. I'm sorry I
                don't know...

SMERALDINA: Smeraldina Tontarosca.

TRUFFALDINO: Of Venice?

SMERALDINA: Unfortunately.

TRUFFALDINO: I know what you mean. Tontarosca. That's a

TRUFFALDINO: (cont'd)
wonderful name.

SMERALDINA: Servants...only three generations. Someone took
a bad turn somewhere. So now you are here in
Venice?

TRUFFALDINO: I know. I can't get used to it. Never thought it
would be so busy. Lot of work here. Growing up
in the Catatoni's home...well...

SMERALDINA: I heard. (gesturing towards the inn) What's this
one like?

TRUFFALDINO: (aside) Now how could I be honest? (to SMERALDINA)
Oh...young and bold.

SMERALDINA: Sounds like mine.

TRUFFALDINO: Really?

SMERALDINA: Demanding...but immature. And that makes them
even more demanding. If you know what I mean?

TRUFFALDINO: I know what you mean. They're almost too privileged.

SMERALDINA: I'd hate to say it but you feel...

TRUFFALDINO: As if you could do a better job?

SMERALDINA: (sarcastic, as masters) Oh! Aren't you the
intelligent one, sir?

TRUFFALDINO: (sarcastic) Why thank you, madam. You needn't say
that.

SMERALDINA: (sarcastic) You're right.

TRUFFALDINO: (sarcastic) Forgive me?

SMERALDINA: Very good!

TRUFFALDINO: I know I know! You too! (realizing they've
clasped hands, hesitates, then, as master) Hands
of a mistress, madam.

SMERALDINA: Palms of a master, sir.

TRUFFALDINO: (as a master) And what delicate objects have these
hands held?

SMERALDINA: (aside) I'd hate to tell him. (to TRUFFALDINO)
Oh sir!

TRUFFALDINO: Any so delicate as...

SMERALDINA: Please don't. Oh. A message for your master.

TRUFFALDINO: And what do you suppose your lady is sending my master?

SMERALDINA: Well I don't know. A message?

TRUFFALDINO: More than a message I'm sure.

SMERALDINA: A secret?

TRUFFALDINO: Warm...

SMERALDINA: A secret of the heart?

TRUFFALDINO: Very good.

SMERALDINA: Well, how did you know? I don't believe you. I wonder if... (they look at each other, thinking of opening it)

TRUFFALDINO: Well, it is your lady's.

SMERALDINA: A secret of the heart? Won't you do the honour?

TRUFFALDINO: The proof is in your hands, my dear Smeraldina.

SMERALDINA: Oh why not?

TRUFFALDINO: Yes?

SMERALDINA: (pretending to read) Oh! I can't believe it! No!

TRUFFALDINO: Am I right? Is it a secret from a warm heart?

SMERALDINA: Ohhhhhhhh...

TRUFFALDINO: You must tell me what it is, Smeraldina.

SMERALDINA: I couldn't read it out loud. Here.

TRUFFALDINO: Oh. To be honest with you...

SMERALDINA: Go ahead, read it.

TRUFFALDINO: The light...isn't quite right...

SMERALDINA: I understand.

TRUFFALDINO: You do?

SMERALDINA: I can't read either.

TRUFFALDINO: Not even a little? You mean?...

SMERALDINA: (laughs to herself) Let's try it together. Maybe
                two servants heads will equal one master's. (starts
                to read slowly) "Dear"... Yes.

TRUFFALDINO: It starts with yes?

SMERALDINA: They always start with "dear".

TRUFFALDINO: Oh. Umm... Smeraldina?

SMERALDINA: Just a moment. I think I've got the next one...

TRUFFALDINO: Please don't think me...

SMERALINDA: Bea! Dear Bea! No. What is it?

TRUFFALDINO: Are you... Do you happen to be...

SMERALDINA: Yes?

TRUFFALDINO: Have you ever been...

SMERALDINA: Oh no. I've been a witness.

TRUFFALDINO: Oh. OH! A witness, eh? Now, Dear Bea!

SMERALDINA: Is that all you wanted to know?

TRUFFALDINO: I think so.

SMERALDINA: "T".

TRUFFALDINO: Yes. It's a "T".

SMERALDINA: "R".

TRUFFALDINO: ...you.

SMERALDINA: "I".

TRUFFALDINO: Oh. (realizing SMERALDINA's still reading)

SMERALDINA: "R,U,I,O"? I don't think so.

TRUFFALDINO: I though you were asking me a question.

SMERALDINA: "R,U,I,O"?

TRUFFALDINO: Yes.

SMERALDINA:	I'm sorry. I didn't realize.
TRUFFALDINO:	Smeraldina?
SMERALDINA:	Truffaldino? (staring at each other)

(PANTALONE enters with BEATRICE)

PANTALONE:	Have you no better place to be, girl?
SMERALDINA:	Oh! This is the place I am to be, sir?
PANTALONE:	What?
SMERALDINA:	Ohhh. I'm sorry, sir. Your daughter...would... like to see you.
PANTALONE:	Now?
BEATRICE:	Another opened letter, Truffaldino?
TRUFFALDINO:	It's not mine, sir.
BEATRICE:	Then whose is it? Why it's mine! One opened letter already and now this. (quickly reads the letter) Look here, Signor Pantalone. It's a letter from your daughter. Warning me of Signor Silvio's mad jealousy.
PANTALONE:	And what do you have to do with this letter, Smeraldina?
SMERALDINA:	Me, sir?
BEATRICE:	Who opened this letter?!
SMERALDINA:	Not me, sir.
TRUFFALDINO:	Are you looking at me, sir?
PANTALONE:	What kind of servant are you, Smeraldina?
SMERALDINA:	A faithful one, sir.
PANTALONE:	A faithful one, eh? I'm very sorry about this Signor Federigo. Come here, you.
SMERALDINA:	The mistress wants me home, sir. (exits quickly)
PANTALONE:	Family business, sir. You must excuse me. Stop!! (exits)
BEATRICE:	Where are you going, Truffaldino?

TRUFFALDINO:	Just trying to walk off the dinner, sir. We do appreciate it.
BEATRICE:	Why did you open the letter?
TRUFFALDINO:	I told you it was Smeraldina, sir.
BEATRICE:	Stop lying to me, Truffaldino.
TRUFFALDINO:	I swear, sir!
BEATRICE:	Stand there!
TRUFFALDINO:	Me, sir?
BEATRICE:	Yes, you sir! Give me your belt.
TRUFFALDINO:	But what will hold my pants, sir?
BEATRICE:	You'll be so bent they won't fall down. Now give me your belt and bend over.
TRUFFALDINO:	Oh sir, this is humiliating!
BEATRICE:	Not any less humiliating than opening up private letters.
TRUFFALDINO:	You don't understand. (she starts to beat him) Oh my, sir! For heaven's sake! No! (aside) How am I doing?
BEATRICE:	Scream! Scream you fool!
TRUFFALDINO:	(screaming) My belt is hurting me, sir!
BEATRICE:	That's better. (finishes beating him) Now if you don't mind? (handing back belt)
TRUFFALDINO:	Would you like to keep it, sir? A souvenir?
BEATRICE:	(she hits him, drops belt) Now let that be a lesson to you. Signor Pantalone... (exits)

(TRUFFALDINO picks up belt)

FLORINDO:	(enters) Truffaldino? What are you doing with that belt?
TRUFFALDINO:	Umm... Oh! (hitting himself with his belt) Punishing myself, sir.
FLORINDO:	You mustn't be so hard on yourself.

TRUFFALDINO: It's my background, sir.

FLORINDO: But why...

TRUFFALDINO: I failed you again so... I couldn't find Pasquale.

FLORINDO: Oh! Well then...let me help you.

TRUFFALDINO: Oh no, sir!

FLORINDO: There. (hits him)

TRUFFALDINO: That's the right spot, sir.

FLORINDO: More?

TRUFFALDINO: No, sir.

FLORINDO: Then let that be a lesson to you, Truffaldino.

TRUFFALDINO: Thank you, sir.

FLORINDO: Now I trust you'll find him?

TRUFFALDINO: I thank you for your faith, sir.

FLORINDO: You're welcome. I haven't had much luck either.
                I have been to the post office...nothing...the
                Lido...the grand canal...nothing. I think I'll
                try the Piazza San Marco. I could use the walk.
                You know all the streets are paved with water,
                Truffaldino?

TRUFFALDINO: It's Venice, sir.

FLORINDO: Perhaps. (exits)

TRUFFALDINO: Good. Was that painful, my darling? My darling?
                Sounds as if she's asleep. Well, to work. Whose
                luggage shall I unpack first? (enters BEATRICE's
                room) Now I'll just take these out. Oh well. I
                don't know about that. Well yes, but really? Oh!
                Well. I know masters do have their own tastes.
                and who am I to know what's in fashion? Oh, what
                is this? A portrait? Oh, isn't he a handsome
                gentleman. Odd. Looks familiar to me. Oh well,
                I've worked for so many they all begin to resemble
                one another.

FLORINDO: (off) Truffaldino?

TRUFFALDINO: (running into other room) Yes, sir.

FLORINDO:	What are you doing?
TRUFFALDINO:	Freshening up your clothes, sir. Back so soon?
FLORINDO:	I forgot my cape. Will you get it for me.
TRUFFALDINO:	Cape, sir?
FLORINDO:	Yes, cape!
TRUFFALDINO:	Here you are, sir.
FLORINDO:	Thank you. Put these letters in my trunk.
TRUFFALDINO:	Certainly, sir. Will you hold this? (indicates the portrait)
FLORINDO:	What's this?
TRUFFALDINO:	What's what, sir?
FLORINDO:	This...
TRUFFALDINO:	Oh...that's just...
FLORINDO:	It's me!
TRUFFALDINO:	You sir?!
FLORINDO:	Me, you fool! The one I gave to my Beatrice. How did you get this?
TRUFFALDINO:	Yes, how did I get this?...
FLORINDO:	Yes!
TRUFFALDINO:	It's mine, sir.
FLORINDO:	Yours?
TRUFFALDINO:	My last master, bless his soul, left it to me.
FLORINDO:	Left it to you?
TRUFFALDINO:	He was in debt to me and left a few lira with this portrait. Have you any idea what you're worth, sir?
FLORINDO:	How long has your master been...gone?
TRUFFALDINO:	Gone?
FLORINDO:	Dead?

TRUFFALDINO: I'd say a week, sir, no more.

FLORINDO: What was your master's name?

TRUFFALDINO: Hard to say, sir.

FLORINDO: The name?

TRUFFALDINO: I don't remember. He travelled in disguise.

FLORINDO: (thinks) In disguise? (aside) Beatrice escaped in her brother's clothes! Your master was young, wasn't he?

TRUFFALDINO: I'd say...yes.

FLORINDO: He didn't shave, did he?

TRUFFALDINO: I'm afraid not, sir.

FLORINDO: (aside) It can't be? (to TRUFFALDINO) Do you know where your master came from?

TRUFFALDINO: Turin, sir?

FLORINDO: (aside) It must be! (to TRUFFALDINO) She's dead? All for nothing. You're sure your young master is dead, Truffaldino?

TRUFFALDINO: I was his servant, sir.

FLORINDO: Oh! How?!

TRUFFALDINO: How?

FLORINDO: How did he die?

TRUFFALDINO: Bad clams?

FLORINDO: Bad clams?!

TRUFFALDINO: It's been a terrible season for clams, sir. First, the infection eats out your intestines, then, the liver, then the...

FLORINDO: Stop! Stop! Where...where was he buried? Ohh!

TRUFFALDINO: Couldn't bury him, sir.

FLORINDO: Not buried?

TRUFFALDINO: Cremated, sir.

FLORINDO: Cremated?!

TRUFFALDINO: No other way to do it, sir. I'm sure you understand?
                 After the disease gets the body, then the coffin,
                 then the rugs...

FLORINDO: Don't say it! (aside) Just like her to do such
                 a thing. And it was all for me! What am I going
                 to do?! (to TRUFFALDINO) Truffaldino, please
                 go!

TRUFFALDINO: May I suggest a nap, sir.

FLORINDO: Go! I need to be alone! (exits into room)

TRUFFALDINO: I wonder if he knew the young master, What's this?...
                 (holding the letters) Oh well, I better get on with
                 my work. I'll give these to him later. (enters
                 BEATRICE's room and opens trunk)

                 (BEATRICE and PANTALONE enter inn)

PANTALONE: If you won't take my wedding suit, may I offer my
                 home on the Adriatic. My late wife and I
                 honeymooned there.

BEATRICE: No, no the money is all I need.

PANTALONE: Please. You must.

BEATRICE: Truffaldino, what are you doing?

TRUFFALDINO: I was going to air your clothes.

BEATRICE: Never mind! Never mind!

PANTALONE: You're nervous. Oh, how charming.

BEATRICE: What are these?

TRUFFALDINO: These? Sir?

BEATRICE: Florindo?! Where did you get these, Truffaldino?!

PANTALONE: I know how you feel. I behaved the same way on
                 my wedding day.

BEATRICE: Please Signor Pantalone... I am asking you,
                 Truffaldino.

TRUFFALDINO: I know you are, sir.

BEATRICE: The letters!

TRUFFALDINO:	Are mine, sir! (aside) Might as well try again.
BEATRICE:	Yours?
TRUFFALDINO:	I inherited them, sir.
BEATRICE:	From whom? I can't believe this!
TRUFFALDINO:	I can't either. My previous master, sir. I was in Venice with this master before travelling to Verona. He died in an awful accident.
BEATRICE:	Died? How did he come to die? Oh please...
TRUFFALDINO:	Drowned, sir.
BEATRICE:	Drowned?
PANTALONE:	Who is this gentleman you are so concerned over, sir?
BEATRICE:	Was his name Florindo, Truffaldino?
TRUFFALDINO:	Could be..
BEATRICE:	NO!
TRUFFALDINO:	I'd say yes, sir.
BEATRICE:	Florindo Aretusi?
TRUFFALDINO:	Flor...in...do Ar...e...tu...si? I'm afraid so, sir.
BEATRICE:	No, not Florindo!
TRUFFALDINO:	Drowned on his way to the Lido, sir. Became upset with the gondolier and decided to take over the gondola himself. At first I thought he was going to overpower the gondolier but then...
BEATRICE:	Then what?
PANTALONE:	Don't just stare at us!
TRUFFALDINO:	He fell overboard, sir. Hit his head against the gondola and sank to the bottom. There was nothing the gondolier could do.
BEATRICE:	Oh Florindo! That's just like him. Always trying to take command! Please God, tell me it's not true!

PANTALONE: Sir? Are you all right?

BEATRICE: My Florindo. He's gone! No! How can it be? I've come this far. I'm here! No, please don't say it! No! Here I am. Disguised as my brother. Wearing my dead brother's clothes. All for you! Florindo! (crying) First my brother...now...

TRUFFALDINO: Close friends, sir?

BEATRICE: How much more can I take? To live when two have died for you. I must die! What better punishment. Oh my heart!

TRUFFALDINO: I have a saying about two hearts, sir. It may comfort you.

BEATRICE: Please! Will you leave me alone!

> (SILVIO appears beside the inn practising his fencing)

Oh no! (exits)

PANTALONE: Is this true, Truffaldino?

TRUFFALDINO: I'm not sure we're thinking about the same thing, sir. What's your truth?

PANTALONE: A woman? Could it be true?

TRUFFALDINO: A woman, sir?

PANTALONE: You idiot! A woman!

TRUFFALDINO: I've been working for a woman, sir?

PANTALONE: Incredible! I've got to tell Clarice.

> (LOMBARDI appears on the opposite side of inn from SILVIO)

LOMBARDI: (whispering) Silvio?

SILVIO: Father.

LOMBARDI: What are you doing?

SILVIO: Practising, Father.

LOMBARDI: You idiot! Come here!

SILVIO: Oh Father! (runs off)

LOMBARDI:	(running to SILVIO) My son, my son!
PANTALONE:	(sees LOMBARDI) Oh! Dr. Lombardi! Great news! Great news! You won't believe it! (runs off following LOMBARDI, following SILVIO)
TRUFFALDINO:	Won't believe it? Who would want to believe it? (looks at stomach and slaps it, then starts to exit I've been working for a woman. Me! Truffaldino Batocchio of Bergamo. Oh my God, I can't even recognize a woman when I see one. I could be tarred and feathered for this! (exits)
BEATRICE:	(alone) Oh death take me quickly!
FLORINDO:	(alone) Soon I will be with you!
BEATRICE:	My darling!
FLORINDO:	My darling!
	(BRIGHELLA, NICKI, and VITTORIO enter. They burst into the rooms. BEATRICE and FLORINDO are simultaneously being pulled out of their rooms backwards. BRIGHELLA is pulling BEATRICE and NICKI and VITTORIO are trying to pull FLORINDO out of his room. BEATRICE and FLORINDO cannot see one another)
BEATRICE:	No! No! I must! Do not hold me back.
BRIGHELLA:	I cannot do that, madam.
NICKI:	Sir, you mustn't!
FLORINDO:	Let me go! Who are you to stop a man from his destiny?!
VITTORIO:	Please, sir. Not near the inn. Think of our reputation.
BEATRICE:	Stand back, Brighella! (throws BRIGHELLA down, he gets up) I said stand back! (throws BRIGHELLA down)
FLORINDO:	I warned you, waiter! Away! (throws him down) Beatrice?
BEATRICE:	Florindo?
FLORINDO:	You're alive?!

BEATRICE: And you?...

FLORINDO: I am! I am! (climbing over NICKI, VITTORIO and
                BRIGHELLA)

BEATRICE: Oh my Florindo!

                        (They fall into each other's arms while
                         NICKI, VITTORIO and BRIGHELLA are trapped
                         on the floor)

FLORINDO: Oh my Beatrice!

BRIGHELLA: Get up, you idiot!

NICKI: I'm trying, sir.

BEATRICE: And I was just about to drown myself!

FLORINDO: Why would you want to do that my love?

BEATRICE: I heard you were drowned.

FLORINDO: Drowned? Who told you such lies?

BEATRICE: My servant.

FLORINDO: Your servant?

BRIGHELLA: Are you all right, sir?

FLORINDO: Of course we're all right! But there is one small
                matter that isn't all right. Our servants. Find
                them, Signor Brighella!

BRIGHELLA: I'll send one of my waiters, sir.

NICKI: Forget it! (runs off)

                        (VITTORIO exits into kitchen)

BRIGHELLA: And if I may say so, I am pleased to be the
                proprietor of the inn you have discovered each other
                in. I don't know what I would have done if we had
                discovered both of you dead.

FLORINDO: Dead? My beloved Beatrice supposedly died of bad
                clams.

BEATRICE: And you, sir, were drowned after wrestling with
                your gondolier.

FLORINDO: Find them, Brighella!

BRIGHELLA:	I will sir. (exits)
BEATRICE:	Oh my Florindo!
FLORINDO:	How long have you been here?
BEATRICE:	Since this morning.
FLORINDO:	No, really? I can't believe we never saw one another.
BEATRICE:	I came here to find you.
FLORINDO:	That I knew. I read your letter from Antonio.
BEATRICE:	How did you get my letter from Antonio?
FLORINDO:	My servant gave it to me by mistake. Said he was carrying it for another. Where are they?
BEATRICE:	I know mine must be about somewhere. He is a difficult one at times.
FLORINDO:	Sounds familiar. Could it be their whole breed is becoming unpredictable?

(BRIGHELLA and TRUFFALDINO enter)

BEATRICE:	Ah! There is one!
BRIGHELLA:	Well we found this one, sir. Now if you'll be so good as to keep an eye on him, we'll go looking for the other.
FLORINDO:	Indeed we will. We must have both. Mustn't we, my dear Beatrice?
BEATRICE:	Certainly we must, my dear Florindo.
BRIGHELLA:	Excuse me, you keep an eye on him. We'll go looking for the other one.
FLORINDO:	Yes, thank you, Brighella!
BRIGHELLA:	Do you know where the other one is?
VITTORIO:	I didn't know there was another, sir.
BRIGHELLA:	Maybe someone in the kitchen knows!
TRUFFALDINO:	Nicki would know!
FLORINDO:	Come back here. Now for a few questions,

	(cont'd)
FLORINDO:	Truffaldino. Where did you find that portrait?

(TRUFFALDINO starts to cry. Stops)

BEATRICE: Florindo! (goes to TRUFFALDINO)

TRUFFALDINO: It's nothing. It's nothing.

FLORINDO: What is it, Truffaldino?

TRUFFALDINO: I don't know if I can, sir. Maybe...privately. If you don't mind, madam? Man to man?

BEATRICE: I understand. Be gentle with him.

FLORINDO: Yes?

TRUFFALDINO: It concerns the servant to your lady, sir. Pasquale.

FLORINDO: You mean the one you fetched the letters for?

TRUFFALDINO: Yes sir. You see, he's the one that's really at fault here. Very bad judgement, my brother.

FLORINDO: Your brother?

TRUFFALDINO: I prefer you don't say a word to your lady. I prefer to take the blame he surely deserves. That idiot!

FLORINDO: What happened?

TRUFFALDINO: Do you remember hearing about those English sheep that were brought into Venice last month?

FLORINDO: English sheep?!

TRUFFALDINO: A very unwise decision if you ask me.

FLORINDO: But what do they have to do with Pasquale? Oh no?!

TRUFFALDINO: Oh yes.

FLORINDO: He didn't?

TRUFFALDINO: He did. Very few women in Venice. Couldn't help himself I'm afraid.

FLORINDO: Why, that's uncouth!

TRUFFALDINO: Not only is it...uncouth, sir, it's horribly couth. Well, he caught a horrible disease as you

TRUFFALDINO:	(cont'd) can well imagine. It affected his brain. Became quite delirious.
FLORINDO:	I can imagine. Those silly ass English. They never stop infecting our society.
TRUFFALDINO	He didn't mean to cause such havoc. He begged me to take the blame for fear your lady would send him away. And of course that would just finish him off. He's recovered now but his self-confidence is very low. Anyway it was I that made up all those stories about the death and your portrait and he... Oh! Your portrait, sir. I would never have known it was your portrait, sir. What have you done to your hair? Is that a wig? Not a bad job.
BEATRICE:	Florindo? Would you please include me in all this? If it's possible?
FLORINDO:	Well I don't know. You see, my dear, your servant..
TRUFFALDINO:	Please sir. Tell your lady it was my fault. Do not... I beg you not say it was Pasquale. Allow me to take his punishment. He couldn't handle anymore I assure you. You see, the sheep he...
FLORINDO:	That's enough! (pause) All right!
TRUFFALDINO:	Better yet, I'll tell her it was my fault.
FLORINDO:	Well...
TRUFFALDINO:	Madam?
BEATRICE:	What have you been telling my signor, Florindo?
TRUFFALDINO:	About the tragedy of his servant Pasquale.
BEATRICE:	Who?
TRUFFALDINO:	My cousin. (aside) Might as well keep it in the family. (starts to wipe a tear away)
BEATRICE:	If it's difficult for you?...
TRUFFALDINO:	I have no one else that I can really confide in, madam. You see it was Pasquale that created all the confusion although he didn't really know what he was doing. And then when he did realize what he was doing, it was too late. He was afraid your Signor Florindo would surely get rid of him.
BEATRICE:	For what?

TRUFFALDINO:	Well, do you remember hearing about that French circus that came through last month?
BEATRICE:	No. But I do remember that a French pox infecting... Could it be?
TRUFFALDINO:	It was!
BEATRICE:	Those French! They never stop! At any cost!
TRUFFALDINO:	Pasquale took up with them one night...
BEATRICE:	In more ways than one I'm sure.
TRUFFALDINO:	You're right.
BEATRICE:	That's awful.
TRUFFALDINO:	Although he recovered from the infection it left him a little... (pointing to his head)
BEATRICE:	Your poor cousin.
TRUFFALDINO:	I was trying to protect him but then he suddenly became delirious and handed me his master's letters. Well there I was. I stupidly made up all those stories for him, madam. Can you forgive me? Please don't say anything to your Florindo about Pasquale, madam? I prefer to take the punishment young Pasquale should really get.
BEATRICE:	Why did you sacrifice yourself?
TRUFFALDINO:	Servant to servant. We have such little protection, madam.
BEATRICE:	So unselfish!
FLORINDO:	Truffaldino, have you told her the whole story?
TRUFFALDINO:	I certainly have.
FLORINDO:	All right. Are you ready for your punishment?
TRUFFALDINO:	Yes sir.
BEATRICE:	My dear Florindo.
FLORINDO:	Yes, my dear Beatrice?
BEATRICE:	Such a fortunate day.
FLORINDO:	Of course it is.

BEATRICE:	And who is to be the victim of our good fortune?
FLORINDO:	Unfortunately Truffaldino.
BEATRICE:	Can we not forgive him? Are we not indebted to him?
FLORINDO:	Oh very well. But one thing Beatrice, your servant
TRUFFALDINO:	(interrupting) I'm deeply grateful and I'm sure Pasquale will feel the same. He'll be so relieved.
BEATRICE:	Now I must go to Signor Pantalone's. Under my brother's will, he is my legal guardian.
FLORINDO:	I also have arrangements that I must complete with my banker. I will join you shortly.
BEATRICE:	I'll wait for you at Signor Pantalone's.
FLORINDO:	Thank you, my love, for understanding.
BEATRICE:	It's you that understands.
FLORINDO:	Oh! I don't think I know where Pantalone lives?
TRUFFALDINO:	Allow me, sir.
FLORINDO:	Oh thank you, Truffaldino.
BEATRICE:	Oh thank you, Truffaldino. (pause) Florindo, is it you?
FLORINDO:	It is, my love! Go, I will see you soon.
BEATRICE:	I hope my trunk will soon be in our room. (exits)
TRUFFALDINO:	Sir?
FLORINDO:	Yes?
TRUFFALDINO:	Would you be so kind as to do me a favour?
FLORINDO:	It depends. What is it?
TRUFFALDINO:	It's love, sir.
FLORINDO:	Don't get involved.
TRUFFALDINO:	But sir?...
FLORINDO:	I know. You can't help it, can you?

RUFFALDINO: Can you, sir?

LORINDO: Of course not. Who is it?

RUFFALDINO: A maid servant to the lady Clarice. The daughter of
               Signor Pantalone. You see, if you could assist me?...

LORINDO: How?

RUFFALDINO: Oh, in arguing my case in front of Signor Pantalone,
               sir.

LORINDO: Is there a case worth arguing?

RUFFALDINO: A wonderful one, sir!

LORINDO: The point is whether she feels the same.

RUFFALDINO: The point is well taken, sir. She does.

LORINDO: Then...

RUFFALDINO: Yes?

LORINDO: I will.

RUFFALDINO: Oh thank you, sir!

                         (SILVIO runs by)

ILVIO: Hello Orazio! Can't stop now. (exits)

LORINDO: Wasn't that?...

                         (LOMBARDI enters)

OMBARDI: (screaming) Silvio, my son! (exits)

RUFFALDINO: (as LOMBARDI runs by) And that's his father.

                         (PANTALONE enters)

ANTALONE: Doctor Lombardi! (exits)

LORINDO: (as PANTALONE runs by) Who's that?

RUFFALDINO: Signor Pantalone, sir.

LORINDO: Isn't that where Beatrice?... (running after
               PANTALONE)

RUFFALDINO: Yes, sir. But the banker, sir?

FLORINDO: To hell with the banker! (exits)

TRUFFALDINO: Is that wise? A master without a banker is like...
               (listens) ...a servant without a master? Oh
               excellent, my darling. Just up?

FLORINDO: (off) Truffaldino!

TRUFFALDINO: Coming, sir!

Act Two, Scene Two

PANTALONE's house.

SMERALDINA: A woman?!

CLARICE: I've told you three times already, Smeraldina.

SMERALDINA: (aside) Could it be true? (to CLARICE) I
               realize that, madam. It's just so difficult for
               me to believe. I've never been fooled by a woman
               before.

CLARICE: But you were and so were we all.

                    (SMERALDINA is giggling to herself)

               What are you laughing at?

SMERALDINA: At another who was fooled, madam.

CLARICE: Silvio, I suppose.

SMERALDINA: Oh no, that's to be expected.

CLARICE: Then whom are you speaking of?

SMERALDINA: May I ask a favour of you, madam?

CLARICE: Only if you tell me who you are laughing at?

SMERALDINA: Truffaldino Batocchio of Bergamo, madam.

CLARICE: Who?

SMERALDINA: Signora Beatrice's servant.

CLARICE: How well do you know him?

SMERALDINA: Only the name so far, madam. Although I feel more.

CLARICE: I understand only too well. Why...do...I...love...
              Silvio? Oh I know, I know... What is it,
              Smeraldina?

SMERALDINA: Is it possible...to...

CLARICE: Yes?

SMERALDINA: Drop our stations for a moment? Please forgive me,
              madam, but, may we speak to one another as...

CLARICE: Friends?

SMERALDINA: As women.

CLARICE: I'd love to. Let's sit down.

SMERALDINA: Thank you, Clarice. Now, hasn't a woman saved
              your marriage?

CLARICE: Yes.

SMERALDINA: Well, that woman may insure my marriage.

CLARICE: To who?

SMERALDINA: To Truffaldino.

CLARICE: Oh? How?

SMERALDINA: If you, another woman, insure mine as well.

CLARICE: I've never been a woman before...

SMERALDINA: Now's your chance, Clarice!

CLARICE: Really? What shall I do?

SMERALDINA: Speak to Signora Beatrice on my behalf, Clarice.
                Woman to woman. Will you do that for me?

CLARICE: I will! I will!

SMERALDINA: Oh thank you, madam!

CLARICE: Are we back to our stations now?

SMERALDINA: I'm afraid so, madam.

CLARICE: Oh. Too bad.

                    (A knock is heard)

                Who could that be?

SMERALDINA: Too soft for your Silvio, madam, I'm sure. (exits)

CLARICE: Oh well then let them in. Oh, perhaps it is Silvio.
                Of course. Come to apologize.

SMERALDINA: Madam? It's the other woman. Signora Beatrice
                Rasponi.

                    (BEATRICE enters dressed as a woman)

BEATRICE: Signora Beatrice Rasponi, madam.

CLARICE: Oh Beatrice!

BEATRICE: Clarice. (they embrace) Is your father here?

CLARICE: I thought he was with you.

BEATRICE: He thought so too until he realized who I was.

CLARICE: He knows.

BEATRICE: He does.

CLARICE: What could that mean, Beatrice?

BEATRICE: That's why I'm here, Clarice.

CLARICE: Did you get my message about Silvio?

BEATRICE: I certainly did.

                    (A door slams)

SMERALDINA: I believe your father is here, madam.

CLARICE: Oh Beatrice!

BEATRICE: Oh?

CLARICE: Not to worry, Beatrice. I will stand by you.
                 (moving toward the entrance)

                      (SILVIO enters)

SILVIO: Stand aside, my foolish bride!

CLARICE: I am not your bride!

SILVIO: You will be after I pierce this impostor's heart.

CLARICE: You mean you know?

SILVIO: It seems I was the only one who knew of this
                 deception.

BEATRICE: Well then, Signor Silvio.

                      (SILVIO notices her)

SILVIO: He can't fool me! Although he fooled this poor
                 unsuspecting waif.

CLARICE: Waif?!

SILVIO: Don't interrupt me! His disguises are not for love
                 but...

BEATRICE: Only for money, sir.

SILVIO: He admits it! See! Do not fear my love! I will
                 avenge your innocent foolishness. Stand ready to
                 take your punishment, Signor Rasponi of Turin!

CLARICE: (grabbing one of his arms) Silvio!

SILVIO: Let go of my arm!

CLARICE: Help me, Smeraldina!

                      (SMERALDINA grabs his other arm)

SILVIO: Two women will never hold me back!
                      (LOMBARDI enters. He doesn't see BEATRICE)

LOMBARDI: But your father will.

SILVIO: Oh Father. Why now?

LOMBARDI: Hand over your sword, Silvio! (taking sword)

SILVIO: But Father?...

LOMBARDI: (to CLARICE, pointing his sword at her) What are

	(cont'd)
LOMBARDI:	you doing to my son?
PANTALONE:	And what are you doing to my daughter, Signor Lombardi?!
SILVIO:	Asking what she did to me?!
PANTALONE:	Oh well, I have good news for you both.
LOMBARDI:	Too late, Signor Pantalone.
PANTALONE:	You will apologize for this behaviour after you hear what I have to say, Dr. Lombardi.
LOMBARDI:	What do you take me for, sir?
PANTALONE:	Family, sir. Now that your daughter-in-law...
LOMBARDI:	Never!
PANTALONE:	Oh yes she will be, sir.
SILVIO:	Never, Father?
LOMBARDI:	Stop antagonizing me, Pantalone! Give her to that young meat from Turin. He deserves her!
PANTALONE:	But sir, you wouldn't say that after I tell you who he really is.
LOMBARDI:	Content! I hear it all over Venice.
PANTALONE:	Why won't you listen to me?!
LOMBARDI:	Come Silvio. I must go now, sir. I needn't get myself upset any longer.
PANTALONE:	I agree with you, Dr. Lombardi.
LOMBARDI:	We never agree on anything nor shall we ever go into an agreement on any measure ever again!
PANTALONE:	Oh go then, you fool!
SILVIO:	But, Signor Pantalone?
LOMBARDI:	You call me fool, sir?
PANTALONE:	If you won't give me one moment of your precious time...
SILVIO:	I'll give you your precious time, sir.

LOMBARDI: Silvio!

PANTALONE: There will be no marriage between Signor Federigo
                 and my daughter. She awaits your hand.

SILVIO: Can it be?!

CLARICE: Oh Silvio!

LOMBARDI: Never. I will not allow my son to marry into this
                 mad family!

SILVIO: Oh Father!

LOMBARDI: Haven't you been dishonoured enough?!

PANTALONE: But Dr. Lombardi...

LOMBARDI: What is it?

PANTALONE: This is Signora Beatrice of Turin, sir.

                         (BEATRICE starts forward)

SILVIO: What?

PANTALONE: Federigo's sister. We were all deceived, sir.

SILVIO: We were?

                         (PANTALONE nods)

                 What?

                         (PANTALONE winks)

CLARICE: Remember the secret, Silvio?

SILVIO: Oh! The secret.

LOMBARDI: More secrets?! Deception! How could you lower
                 yourself to such behaviour, Silvio?

SILVIO: Don't you understand, Father?

LOMBARDI: I do, Silvio. But understanding does not mean I
                 shall agree...

SILVIO: Oh Father!

LOMBARDI: We are now going!

SILVIO: Please!

(FLORINDO enters)

LOMBARDI:	Shut up!
FLORINDO:	Excuse me!
BEATRICE:	Florindo!
SILVIO:	Orazio! You must help me!
FLORINDO:	I'm sorry about this intrusion, sir. The door was open.
SMERALDINA:	(aside) That's fine... There are no secrets in this house.
FLORINDO:	Are you the master of this gracious home, sir?
PANTALONE:	I am.
FLORINDO:	It is a pleasure to finally meet the great merchant of Venice, Signor Pantalone.
LOMBARDI:	This is a friend of yours?
SILVIO:	It is, Father.
PANTALONE:	It might also be a pleasure to me, sir, when you tell me who you are?
FLORINDO:	Florindo Aretusi of Turin.
BEATRICE:	My fiancé, Signor Pantalone.
PANTALONE:	Your fiancé? Ahh!
SILVIO:	Is that true, Orazio?
FLORINDO:	I'm sorry for the deception, Silvio.
LOMBARDI:	Another deception? What kind of people do you attract, Silvio?
FLORINDO:	Signor Pantalone, I understand you are the legal guardian of my fiancé Beatrice Rasponi.
PANTALONE:	I am, sir.
FLORINDO:	You would do us a great honour, sir, if you would allow me to take over your guardianship by giving me her hand in marriage.
PANTALONE:	I wish I could, sir. But, it was revealed to me

PANTALONE:	(cont'd) when Signora Beatrice revealed herself to me, that is...that her brother would not have done so.
FLORINDO:	That's true, sir.
BEATRICE:	But it was love, sir!
PANTALONE:	But was it not love that your brother had for you?
BEATRICE:	Not the love that knows when to give love away, sir.
PANTALONE:	True, Signora Beatrice. And the love you have for Signor Aretusi was also revealed to me when you revealed yourself to me, that is.
LOMBARDI:	Excuse me, Signor Pantalone. Revealed to me when you revealed yourself to me, that is?
PANTALONE:	Yes.
LOMBARDI:	Thank you.
FLORINDO:	Well sir?
BEATRICE:	Signor Pantalone. I cannot live without Florindo!
PANTALONE:	Now there, Silvio, is true devotion.
SILVIO:	Thank you, Signor Pantalone! Did you hear that, Clarice?
FLORINDO:	Then you will agree, sir.
PANTALONE:	I will. But it would be a dishonour to my family if I didn't allow the same agreement for my daughter.
CLARICE:	Oh, Papa!
SILVIO:	You must agree, Father!
PANTALONE:	Dr. Lombardi?
LOMBARDI:	Signor Pantalone?
BEATRICE:	Sir?
FLORINDO:	Doctor?
CLARICE:	(coming over to LOMBARDI) Father?

PANTALONE: Now, Dr. Lombardi, what would your poor wife think? May she rest in peace.

LOMBARDI: How dare you! What about your poor wife?

PANTALONE: She would welcome our new son.

LOMBARDI: Well...I welcome my new daughter!

SILVIO: Oh thank you, Father.

LOMBARDI: What did I say?

PANTALONE: Welcome...

LOMBARDI: I did? What have I done?

CLARICE: Silvio!

SILVIO: Clarice!

(They embrace)

BEATRICE: Clarice?

CLARICE: Oh dear Beatrice! Congratulations!

BEATRICE: We were partners to the end, weren't we?

SILVIO: Will you please forgive me, madam?

BEATRICE: Duels are not easily forgotten, sir.

SILVIO: My own foolishness, madam. Orazio, it is your lady who nearly killed me, sir. I was trying to attack my father-in-law.

BEATRICE: Killed? I saved your life!

PANTALONE: Absolutely, Silvio.

SILVIO: And I thank you, madam. I hope I have the same honour one day.

LOMBARDI: To save your own life?

SILVIO: Yes, Father.

PANTALONE: Now then, are all the apologies in order? Have we settled our disagreements? Can we now consider all

LOMBARDI: A family?

PANTALONE: That's very kind of you, Dr. Lombardi.

LOMBARDI: I know, Signor Pantalone.

SMERALDINA: Is it over?

                          (TRUFFALDINO enters. Sneezes from having
                          fallen in the canal)

                 Oh bless him.

PANTALONE: How did you?...

TRUFFALDINO: I'm sorry. I knocked the open door, sir. I assume
                 you were expecting me.

PANTALONE: Were we?

FLORINDO: What is it, Truffaldino?

TRUFFALDINO: (whispering to FLORINDO) Sir?

SMERALDINA: (whispering) Madam.

FLORINDO: Oh yes. Signor Pantalone?

PANTALONE: Yes?

FLORINDO: Would you do me the honour of a favour, sir?

PANTALONE: How can I serve you?

FLORINDO: My servant...would like to marry your servant.

SMERALDINA: (aside) Who's he talking about?!

PANTALONE: I see no obstacle to this union. What do you say
                 Smeraldina?

SMERALDINA: Ummm...if you think he would be worthy, sir?

PANTALONE: Worthy, sir?

FLORINDO: Oh, more than worthy, sir.

SMERALDINA: Madam?!

CLARICE: Right. If I may interrupt, sirs.

FLORINDO: By all means, madam.

CLARICE: I have promised Smeraldina to Signora Beatrice's
                 servant.

BEATRICE: You have?

FLORINDO:	You already promised her to someone, madam?
CLARICE:	Yes sir. However, if Smeraldina is your servant's wish?...
FLORINDO:	No no, please exclude mine, madam.
CLARICE:	Oh no, no, it is mine I should exclude, sir.
FLORINDO:	Oh, no, no, no...
BEATRICE:	My dear Florindo? Who is it you are excluding?
FLORINDO:	My servant.
BEATRICE:	Oh well then, Smeraldina will marry Truffaldino.
SMERALDINA:	(aside) Oh bless her.
FLORINDO:	No, she shall marry Pasquale.
SMERALDINA:	(aside) Will I now have two?
BEATRICE:	Not if you are excluding your servant.
FLORINDO:	But my servant is...
FLORINDO:	(simultaneously) Truffaldino.
BEATRICE:	(simultaneously) Pasquale.
TRUFFALDINO:	At your service.
FLORINDO:	(simultaneously) Pasquale?
BEATRICE:	(simultaneously) Truffaldino?
TRUFFALDINO:	Same again.
LOMBARDI:	Excuse me?
PANTALONE:	Just a moment, Dr. Lombardi.
SILVIO:	I think I've got it.
LOMBARDI:	You do? Rubbish!
SMERALDINA:	(to TRUFFALDINO) I don't believe it.
TRUFFALDINO:	Don't.
FLORINDO:	Truffaldino!

TRUFFALDINO: Yes, sir?

     (Pause)

FLORINDO: Now my dear Beatrice, where is your servant?

BEATRICE: There.

TRUFFALDINO: And why not? (no reponse) Didn't I do a good job?
     (no reponse) And who was responsible for getting
     you lovers back together? Me. Truffaldino Pasquale
     Battochio. And if you ask me...

BEATRICE
& FLORINDO: Yes?

TRUFFALDINO: Well...

ALL: Yes?

TRUFFALDINO: I feel as if I've been here before.

ALL: What?!

TRUFFALDINO: I feel I deserve a reward. For it was love that
     surely caused all this confusion. And it would be
     less confusing to us all if you would let me have
     the hand of my dear Smeraldina. She is all that I
     ask.

SMERALDINA: Sir?

TRUFFALDINO: Sir?

PANTALONE: (to FLORINDO) Sir?

SMERALDINA: Madam?

BEATRICE: Florindo?

FLORINDO: If you wish.

     (BRIGHELLA enters not seen)

PANTALONE: Dr. Lombardi. Signor Florindo, Signora Beatrice,
     Dr. Lombardi, Silvio, and my dear, dear Clarice,
     will you all do me the honour of accompanying me
     to Signor Brighella's to celebrate our mutual
     agreements?

FLORINDO: Signor Pantalone? Is that the only place to eat in
     Venice?

BEATRICE:	(the only one who sees Brighella) Florindo! That' very generous of you, sir.
LOMBARDI:	Generous? What do you think they'll be serving, si
PANTALONE:	I'd be afraid to think, Dr. Lombardi. (laughs, notices BRIGHELLA) Oh!
FLORINDO:	May I, my love?
BEATRICE:	Of course, my dear Florindo.
PANTALONE:	Shall we go? Clarice?
CLARICE:	Coming Papa!
SILVIO:	(to PANTALONE while exiting) Papa!

(LOMBARDI and CLARICE hit SILVIO)

PANTALONE:	(exiting) Tell me Brighella. What was in that Venetian sundae?

(All exit except SMERALDINA and TRUFFALDINO

SMERALDINA:	Aren't you the intelligent one, sir?
TRUFFALDINO:	Why thank you, madam. You needn't say that.
SMERALDINA:	You're right. Forgive me.

(Both bow to each other)

TRUFFALDINO:	Madam? (offering his hand)
SMERALDINA:	Sir?

(Both laugh)

TRUFFALDINO:	Smeraldina?
SMERALDINA:	Truffaldino? (about to kiss)
TRUFFALDINO:	(to stomach) Not now, my darling!
SMERALDINA:	Oh?
TRUFFALDINO:	Yes now.

The End

FAVORITE
BROADWAY COMEDIES
from
SAMUEL FRENCH, INC.

BAREFOOT IN THE PARK – BEDROOM FARCE – BLITHE SPIRIT – BUTTERFLIES ARE FREE – CALIFORNIA SUITE – CHAMPAGNE COMPLEX – CHAPTER TWO – COME BLOW YOUR HORN – DA – THE GINGERBREAD LADY – GOD'S FAVORITE – THE GOOD DOCTOR – HAPPY BIRTHDAY, WANDA JUNE – HAY FEVER – HOW THE OTHER HALF LOVES – I OUGHT TO BE IN PICTURES – JUMPERS – KNOCK KNOCK – LAST OF THE RED HOT LOVERS – MY FAT FRIEND – NEVER TOO LATE – NIGHT AND DAY – THE NORMAN CONQUESTS – NORMAN, IS THAT YOU? – THE ODD COUPLE – OTHERWISE ENGAGED – THE OWL AND THE PUSSYCAT – THE PRISONER OF 2ND AVENUE – THE PRIVATE EAR AND THE PUBLIC EYE – THE RAINMAKER – SAME TIME, NEXT YEAR – THE SHOW OFF – 6 RMS RIV VU – THE SUNSHINE HOUSAND CLOWNS – TRAVESTIES – GS – TWO FOR THE SEASAW

s of these and all our plays, consult our Basic lays.

THE
SAMUEL
FRENCH
THEATER
BOOKSHOP

*Specializing in plays and
books on the theater*

ISBN 0 573 61897 6

#21080

O6-DCT-268